SCHOOLS
FOR CITIES
URBAN
STRATEGIES

**National Endowment
for the Arts**

Washington, DC

The Mayors' Institute
on City Design

Sharon Haar editor
Mark Robbins series editor

Distributed by:
Princeton Architectural Press
37 East Seventh Street
New York, New York 10003

For a free catalog of books, call 1.800.722.6657.
Visit our web site at www.papress.com.

© 2002 National Endowment for the Arts and
The Board of Trustees of the University of Illinois
05 04 03 02 4 3 2 1 First Edition

Design by M. Christopher Jones, The VIA Group LLC.

Printed and bound in the United States of America.

Library of Congress Cataloging-In-Publication
Data is available from the National Endowment
for the Arts.

ISBN 1-56898-378-6

NEA Series on Design

Other titles available in this series:

The Mayors' Institute:
Excellence in City Design

Sprawl and Public Space:
Redressing the Mall

University-Community
Design Partnerships:
Innovations in Practice

Your Town:
Mississippi Delta

Front cover:
The Kirk Middle School
in East Cleveland, Ohio,
one of the city's most
important landmarks,
was effectively condemned
by the state's two-thirds
rule. It has since been
demolished (see p. 32 for
details).

Contents

I

Essays

Preface	1
Mark Robbins	
Schools for Cities:	3
Urban Strategies	
Sharon Haar	
Acknowledgments	12
Sharon Haar	
Reenvisioning Schools:	14
The Mayors' Questions	
Leah Ray	

Why Johnny Can't Walk	26
to School	
Constance E. Beaumont	
Lessons from the	34
Chicago Public Schools	
Design Competition	
Cindy S. Moelis with	
Beth Valukas	
Something from "Nothing":	42
Information Infrastructure	
in School Design	
Sheila Kennedy	

An Architect's Primer for	52
Community Interaction	
Julie Eizenberg	
The City of Learning:	60
Schools as Agents for	
Urban Revitalization	
Roy Strickland	
Education and the	70
Urban Landscape:	
Illinois Institute of	
Technology	
Peter Lindsay Schaudt	

II

Case Studies

Prototypes and Paratypes:	78
Future Studies	
Sharon Haar	
Lick-Wilmerding High	84
School, San Francisco	
Pfau Architecture Ltd.	
Architecture of Adjustment,	86
New York City	
kOnyk Architecture	
Booker T. Washington	88
School for the Performing	
and Visual Arts, Dallas	
Allied Works Architecture Inc.	
Camino Nuevo Middle	90
School, Los Angeles	
Daley, Genik Architects	
Elementary School	92
Prototypes, Chicago Public	
Schools	
OWP/P Architects	

Bibliography	96
Image Credits	97
Contributors	98
MICD Session Participants	100
Endnotes	101

I am glad to be here—glad to be part of this dialogue—because I truly know schools can more effectively become not just occasions to help community development but also opportunities to revitalize neighborhoods and communities within our cities and towns. One of the things we have to be mindful about in education is our predisposition to assume that a solution in one circumstance can flow to another situation. There are no silver bullets. An example is the current discussion around school units and small schools. If you do not hold quality constant, it does not matter how much you reduce class size or how small the school unit may be. There are some constants that we have to observe before we actually engage in what will, I think, matter.

—Clifford B. Janey
Superintendent
Rochester Public Schools
MICD Participant

Preface

Mark Robbins
Director of Design, National Endowment for the Arts

The Mayors' Institute on City Design was established by the National
Endowment for the Arts in 1986 to help mayors improve the design and
livability of their cities through intensive sessions with design professionals. In recent years, it has also provided a structure for addressing specific
issues that have an impact on urban development. Some of these specialized sessions have been accomplished through partnerships with other
federal agencies such as the EPA, GSA, and HUD to establish conversations between elected officials and these agencies, which are prime forces
in the public environment. Such collaborations allow Arts Endowment
programs to be a conduit for better design.

As part of a series of four new Leadership Initiatives, the NEA
funded one of these special sessions to identify ways in which schools can
operate as catalysts for community redevelopment. The three-day event
was hosted by the University of Illinois at Chicago (UIC) in March 2000
and included discussions of case studies involving historical schools in
downtown centers, school reuse in suburban settings, and the design of
new school buildings. This book is an outgrowth of that session and a
public forum that followed it. The publication features many examples of
the schools, approaches to teaching, and progressive policies that were
presented there. Many of these projects succeed in bringing architects
together with educators to create the best places for learning.

The efforts to find new methods and forms for school buildings also include a recent design competition for schools in Chicago, sponsored by Business and Professional People for the Public Interest (BPI) and also among the projects discussed here. It was heartening to watch this competition process unfold and, in its aftermath, to hear the comments from some of those in the positions of client and sponsor. They speak in positive terms about architecture and encourage the understanding that design adds value to building. Sunny Fischer of The Richard H. Driehaus Foundation aptly described the mission of the project to "develop exciting and ethical designs and design solutions to the issues that face us today, combining universal design, small schools, and green design." Mike Mayo, a member of the Chicago Public Schools Board of Trustees, detailed pragmatic requirements, as well as the need for the architects' vision. He was, he said, impressed with "their passion for education, their understanding of people, their genuine concern for improving the lives of our children and our families." Given the opportunity to take a critical role in public work, architects have the potential to make a remarkable difference. Aspirations for a democratic nation of well-educated individuals rest on the sort of efforts that the designers, educators, and public officials in this publication have ably demonstrated.

I'd like to thank all of the people who were responsible for hosting this Mayors' Institute on City Design dedicated to schools. Sharon Haar, the coordinator of the project at UIC, brought intelligence and breadth to the endeavor and put together an admirable program to complement the work of the Mayors' Institute sessions. Dean Judith Russi Kirshner, Katerina Rüedi Ray, and Jane M. Saks at UIC insured that the event was supported in the most generous way and integrated it in the curriculum of the College of Architecture and the Arts and the city's cultural institutions. I offer a particular note of gratitude to The Richard H. Driehaus Foundation and Executive Director Sunny Fischer, as well as to the Graham Foundation for Advanced Studies in the Fine Arts and Executive Director Richard Solomon, for their continuing involvement with NEA design initiatives. Finally, I recognize Sharon Haar's careful oversight of this publication and join her in thanking all those who assisted in bringing it to print.

Schools for Cities: Urban Strategies

Sharon Haar
School of Architecture, University of Illinois at Chicago

> There shall be reserved the lot No. 16 of every township, for the
> maintenance of public schools within the said township.
> —The Continental Congress,
> *Land Ordinance of 1785*

> The citizen of the United States does not acquire his practical sci-
> ence and his positive notions from books; the instruction he has
> acquired may have prepared him for receiving those ideas, but it
> did not furnish them. The American learns to know the laws by
> participating in the act of legislation; and he takes a lesson in the
> forms of government from governing. The great work of society
> is ever going on before his eyes and, as it were, under his hands.
> —Alexis de Tocqueville,
> *Democracy in America*, 1835

Throughout United States history, educators and community leaders have
linked democracy and a healthy civic life with the architecture of the
nation's school buildings. As schools represent significant outlays of capital and are major components of the nation's physical, economic, social,
and cultural infrastructure, there exists an ongoing conversation and
debate about the place of education in the development of cities and
urban life. In one sense, this effort is a measure of both national failure
and success. Failure in that the country continues to struggle to provide
adequate environments for learning. Success in that each generation challenges itself to create spaces and buildings appropriate to the educational
needs of its time.

The essays that form the core of this volume derive from a conference held in the spring of 2000. Schools as Catalysts for Community Development was a national session of the Mayors' Institute on City Design (MICD) cosponsored by the National Endowment for the Arts, the American Architectural Foundation, The U.S. Conference of Mayors, and the University of Illinois at Chicago. With an aim to integrate political leadership, social development, and purposeful school design, the conference brought to one event regional and national partners concerned with the design of educational facilities and the critical roles these institutions play in the formation of our nation's diversifying communities and expanding cities. Mayors have greatest control over planning and public policy in their cities, and the potential to shape educational mission can only be made more effective with the inclusion of careful and intentional school design. The events of the MICD afforded an opportunity to bring together mayors, school superintendents, and design professionals to discuss how schools function as both civic institutions and urban infrastructure within the realm of urban planning and development policy.

A 1999 *Chicago Tribune* article noted that in that year alone $16.3 billion would be spent to complete new, expanded, or rehabilitated schools across the United States. The new funds available make this a crucial moment, yet politicians face great challenges: whether to put funds into educational reform, technology, or buildings; whether to renovate older buildings or commit to new buildings; whether to plan for growth or decline in population; and how to resolve the legacies of racism, exacerbated by the physical state of the urban environment. Debbie Moore, a spokeswoman for the Council of Educational Facility Planners, was quoted as saying: "More and more we are seeing health clinics, YMCAs, daycare centers, and public libraries opening up inside our schools. Schools, once again, are becoming the center of our communities."[1] A focus of the MICD's discussion, and a key element in several essays in this volume, is the question of how schools can be specifically designed to serve as centers of their communities. As Jeanne Silver Frankl of the Public Education Association has noted: "If community agencies locate their services on the school site, a more comprehensive approach can be taken to meet the economic, physical, educational, and social needs of individuals and of the community. Additionally, the school, as a locus of positive activity, can serve as a catalyst for strengthening and revitalizing the entire community."[2] Citizens in a wide range of roles are demonstrating a commitment to a diverse array of new educational institutions in urban and suburban settings. Several of the participating mayors, as well as Clifford B. Janey, the superintendent of the Rochester Public Schools, who served as a member of the resource team, discussed examples of the way in which their own school districts are incorporating the facilities described by Moore.

Despite strong community commitments to education, we often approach urban issues with a "crisis mindset" that does not afford the opportunity for critical reflection, or what might be considered careful planning, about the role that design can play in rethinking the consequences of both successful and failing urban environments. When problems become codified as "crises," we should not be surprised if design is redefined as crisis management. Writing against a proposal to bring in the Army Corps of Engineers to design and construct new schools for Los Angeles, the architectural theorist Anthony Vidler hit on the centrality of architecture to education:

> Architecture is not simply concerned with the technical details of planning and construction but, most important, with the relations between the envisioned curriculum and the space in which it is put into practice. The architect plays a crucial role in the consideration of the complex relations between a large institution and its neighborhood, of the careful responses in scale and spatial layout to the needs of teachers and children, of the very materials out of which a good learning environment is built....the architect can serve as catalyst and collaborator, conscience and coordinator.[3]

These crises occur when the design of the city is reduced to an infrastructure problem rather than an institutional opportunity. In the best of circumstances, institutional and infrastructural concerns intersect. The mayors who chose to participate in the MICD session on schools recognized that their task went beyond the repair of warehouses for education.

They were seeking ways to reincorporate schools into the civic life of their cities.

Education theorists consistently speak to the issue of the environment, including the urban environment, in which education should take place. Throughout the sessions of the MICD, architect Julie Eizenberg and school superintendent Clifford Janey spoke of the importance of teaching both "inside" and "outside," by which they meant both in the school and in its community. It is equally important that the school enhance the urban community, not simply as an aesthetic object, but as a site for programmatic development, neighborhood resource development, and urban restructuring. Commitments to school design and planning are as often decisions about urban form and structure as about architectural style and context. The reuse of buildings can restructure the civic orientation of a city: the conversion of disused buildings into schools, the creation of new "downtown" magnet schools, and the transformation of existing schools into shared civic spaces. The mayors from Wichita, Kansas, and Lynn, Massachusetts, both put forward proposals of this nature. Projects such as Roy Strickland's "City of Learning" and preservation concerns raised by Constance Beaumont, both discussed in this book, illustrate concrete ways of bringing these proposals to fruition. They also demonstrate the role of schools as institutions of urban transformation, not only as monuments to pedagogical routines.

When the nation's founders set aside the 16th section of townships to produce funds to build schools, there was no curriculum, no image, and no clearly defined student body for these schools. Our core educational values date back to the days of the early republic, a predominantly agricultural environment. But much of the large-scale impetus for the development of a national public school system came through urban, industrial growth and then postindustrial decentralization. More than any institution of civic life, educational facilities are highly subject to the ebb and flow of demographics: "natural" population rises and falls; local shifts occur between cities, suburbs, and exurbs; and migration and immigration bring new life to cities. But educational values change as well, and with them the expansion of curriculum and the numbers of students pursuing preschool and college preparatory programs, which put even greater pressure on existing school facilities.

In the early 20th century, architects such as Dwight H. Perkins began the movement to design public schools as urban neighborhood centers tied to the dense urban fabric.[4] The idea of the school as a tool of social reform is not new. The workings of such schools—the mass production of a minimally educated population and the building of petit-monuments to the acquisition of specifically American knowledge—are a legacy of early 20th-century urban ideals. At the same time, however, educational leaders such as John Dewey began to focus on the child as a learning being, rather than an empty vessel for the reception of American values or the trained tool of industrial productivity.[5] The continuing reconfiguration of the landscape, from dense cities into large urban regions, compels us to rebuild and more fully utilize these vital institutions of democratic life.

The accessibility of large quantities of undeveloped land allowed suburban schools to take on more "campuslike" forms. Streetcar and railroad suburbs could not have been conceived without the development of schools to absorb the youth of this family-centered culture. After World War II, schools were an important component in the planning of the Levittown communities. Developer William Levitt stated the case succinctly: "A school has to be ready when the house is ready. It's as important as a water main."[6] The sociologist Herbert Gans discovered that the politics of education created the greatest conflict among the Levittowners.[7] Indeed, in postwar America, schools, and particularly the distance to them, were a critical component of the neighborhood unit.[8] To the extent that urban diversity existed, schools were this diversity's common denominator. To the extent that segregation would be extended, despite legislation to the contrary, unequal education would be built into the lower quality of schools in dense, African American districts. The urban school's greatest fault, it was thought, was its location in an urban environment.

Today, the need to provide school buildings no longer revolves purely around school-age population growth and decline; to be viable community facilities, schools must be designed and built to tie directly into the needs and desires of the communities that they serve, both programmatically and physically, in their scale and their symbolic potential to give identity and purpose to the surrounding community. *Schools for Cities: Urban Strategies* addresses these multiple issues as they relate to community development, diversification, and revitalization.

Schools are once again becoming vital community anchors. Educational institutions provide facilities that are critical to urban design such as auditoriums, libraries, and recreational facilities. As landscape architect Peter Lindsay Schaudt emphasizes, as urban institutions, schools should be part of the larger landscape plan for the city. Architect Sheila Kennedy discusses the role of schools as providers of 21st century technological and physical infrastructure. New school buildings offer opportunities to think about urban diversification, the reconfiguration of urban space, the quality and expansion of landscape, and the provision of new spaces for contemporary urban programming. Increasingly, educators and designers recognize that education takes place throughout the community in spaces other than traditional school buildings. Both Julie Eizenberg, discussing a private school, and Roy Strickland, discussing public schools, share examples of techniques to create such community interactions through design. Where they exist, historic buildings provide opportunities to renovate existing urban fabric, and educational programming can also revitalize abandoned urban buildings. Constance Beaumont provides techniques to encourage the preservation of existing school stock in lieu of the building of new "sprawl schools" outside of the existing urban fabric. Beaumont's discussion focuses on the ways in which the preservation of existing buildings, whether schools or otherwise, can serve to preserve the urban fabric, a sense of community, and entire neighborhoods.

Amid the 1990s scrutiny of education nationwide, including the call for new national standards and education reform, a number of educational theorists and practitioners, in the tradition of Dewey, began to look seriously once again at the environment in which education takes place, particularly in large, anonymous, and highly bureaucratic urban school districts such as New York, Boston, and Chicago. While many "small school" experiments first took place in existing school buildings, the small school movement has begun to have a significant impact on school size and form.[9] But, even as many of these new schools have been brought down to scale and incorporate new technologies and specialized curricula, the time of the "mega-school" is not over. This is not to deride the idea of the "campus" school as a concept but to question its particular appropriateness within existing urban settings. In Strickland's "curriculum," for example, the city is the map or text for learning; its buildings, the school. Developments such as these rely, in large measure, on the ability to develop educational partnerships between school districts, community and governmental organizations, and private enterprises. The essay on Chicago's School Design competition demonstrates just such an alliance to create two new schools in Chicago.[10] Several of the mayors who participated in the MICD schools session saw ways in which new schools could provide the impetus for private development of new technology infrastructures in their cities.

Educational institutions provide opportunities to educate today's students about neighborhood and community development. Schools such as New York's "School for the Physical City" are contemporary versions of design and planning education once provided through textbooks. Examples include Chicago's *Wacker Manual*, intended to educate Chicago's students to support the implementation of the 1909 plan for Chicago, or my immigrant grandmother's 1923 edition of *Our City: New York*, a book written by students of New York City's public schools. As architectural critic Mildred Friedman wrote in the 1970s: "One way to make the process of learning 'action rich' is to move our isolated children out of the school buildings into the community. This cannot be accomplished with an occasional field trip to a museum or to the zoo. To be effective, this process means actually locating elements or aspects of school in the community."[11] The needs of today's diverse constituencies and communities are different from those of earlier generations; this diversity should be reflected in and supported by our educational institutions. Schools remain the locus for education that supports community

Teachers are introduced to the Chicago Plan, 1919.

New York City kindergarten children learn about city planning, 1924.

building in both the figurative the and literal sense.

This book does not endeavor to offer a model curriculum, model building, or a specific prescription for urban or educational form or reform. In an important sense, all education remains local. Instead, *Schools for Cities: Urban Strategies* offers essays and case studies that illustrate diverse ways in which educational and urban development can be conjoined. This is of critical importance in the context of a heated and increasingly divisive national debate on education reform, increased capital spending on school construction and renovation, and active discourse on the quality of life and design in our cities and communities. New private and public partnerships, community coalitions, and curricular innovation involving community participation provide organizational models for the physical reintegration of schools into urban revitalization. The essays that follow, first "The Mayors' Questions" and then the essays offered by members of the resource team, begin to demonstrate the ways in which school design can become part of an overall urban strategy. Finally, in the spirit of the proposition that "one size does not fit all," the book concludes with a series of case studies illustrating recent school projects that take up the challenge of city design.

Acknowledgments

Schools for Cities: Urban Strategies began as a national session of the Mayors' Institute on City Design (MICD)—Schools as Catalysts for Community Development—held at the University of Illinois at Chicago (UIC) in March 2000. A program originated and funded by the National Endowment for the Arts (NEA), the MICD is now carried out in partnership with The U.S. Conference of Mayors and administered by the American Architectural Foundation. Continuing support of this critical interface between city governments and design professionals creates a unique and vital public forum. I would like to thank Mark Robbins, Director of Design at the NEA, for recognizing Chicago as a location from which to launch a discussion of urban schools, design, and development, as well as Christine Saum and her staff at the MICD. I would also like to thank and congratulate the mayors, as well as their staffs, and school superintendents for their willingness to engage their cities in a dialogue about design and members of the resource team for their expertise and good will.

The conference would not have taken place without the financial and additional support of foundations, agencies, and individuals around Chicago: The Richard H. Driehaus Foundation, Fannie Mae Foundation, Graham Foundation for Advanced Studies in the Fine Arts, The City of Chicago Department of Cultural Affairs, and The Chicago Public Library. The conference was generously supported through the Office of the Provost, the College of Architecture and the Arts, and the School of Architecture at UIC. Dean of the College Judith Russi Kirshner and then Director of the School of Architecture Katerina Rüedi Ray were active participants in the organization and activities of the conference. Other important participants included Leah Ray, the Program Director, Stephen R. Bruns, a graduate research assistant, and many students, who always have the generosity and curiosity to pitch in. Special thanks are due to Jane M. Saks, Director of Advancement in the College of Architecture and the Arts, for her role in helping to conceptualize the initiative and bringing together allies throughout Chicago devoted to design and education.

Stephen Sennott was instrumental to the early phases of editing this book, as were Rose Grayson, a Master of Architecture student at UIC, M. Christopher Jones at The VIA Group, Ann Bremner, and Jennifer Thompson at Princeton Architectural Press in the later stages. Finally, the many contributors to this book, Mark Robbins at the NEA, the authors of the essays, and the firms and individuals who contributed to the case studies should be recognized for their devotion to the cause of cities, schools, and the education of urban youth.

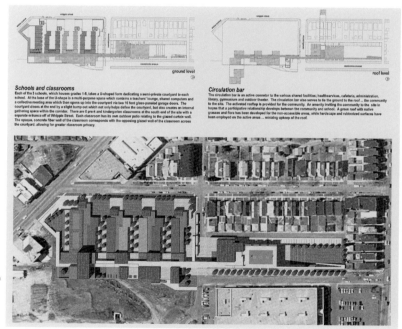

ground level

roof level

Schools and classrooms
Each of the 3 schools, which houses grades 1-8, takes a U-shaped form dedicating a semi-private courtyard to each school. At the base of the U-shape is a multi-purpose space which contains a teachers' lounge, shared computers and a collective meeting area which then opens up into the courtyard via two 16 foot glass-paneled garage doors. The courtyard closes at the end by a slight bump out which not only helps define the courtyard, but also creates an internal gathering space within the corridor. There are 6 pre-k and kindergarten classrooms at the south end of the site with a separate entrance off of Whipple Street. Each classroom has its own outdoor patio relating to the glazed curtain wall. The opaque, concrete fiber wall of the classroom corresponds with the opposing glazed wall of the classroom across the courtyard, allowing for greater classroom privacy.

Circulation bar
The circulation bar is an active connector to the various shared facilities; health services, cafeteria, administration, library, gymnasium and outdoor theater. The circulation bar also serves to tie the ground to the roof ... the community to the site. The activated rooftop is provided for the community. An amenity inviting the community to the site in hopes that a participative relationship develops between the community and school. A green roof with native grasses and flora has been developed for the non-accessible areas, while hardscape and rubberized surfaces have been employed on the active areas ... minizing upkeep of the roof.

David Dodt and Greg Lauterbach, Master of Architecture final project for the Chicago Public Schools Competition North Side site. Faculty: Xavier Vendrell and Dan Wheeler, School of Architecture, UIC, 2002.

Rogers School
Mayors' Institute on City Design

Reenvisioning Schools: The Mayors' Questions

Leah Ray
School of Architecture, University of Illinois at Chicago

Mayors are rarely architects, yet mayors have a profound influence upon the architecture of their cities. In the process of raising funds, negotiating with constituents, and determining where schools will be built, architecture is often an afterthought. The goal of the Mayors' Institute on City Design: Schools as Catalysts for Community Development was to ask mayors to spend a weekend focusing on architecture, so that these urban policymakers could become more aware of the potential effects of architecture on community development.

Public presentation: Jane Tompkins, Avram Lothan, William Ayers, and Carol Ross Barney

Julie Eizenberg and Merrill Elam speaking with D'Arcy Dixon Pignanelli of Murray City, Utah

Clifford B. Janey and Sharon Haar

Clifford B. Janey speaking with school superintendents from participating cities

Rogers School Stamford, Connecticut

Downtown Lynn, Massachusetts

The thesis that structured the conversations that took place during the Chicago Mayors' Institute was the potential of school architecture not only to enhance education but also to catalyze community development. Educators and architects agree: the architecture of schools profoundly affects the experiences of the students and teachers who inhabit them.[1] Furthermore, physical design of a school can boost the development of a struggling community. How can mayors, as leaders of their cities, bring architecture into their educational vision?

Each of the mayors participating in the symposium came to the table with a set of questions regarding specific schools in their own cities. These questions often had to do with the ideal size or location of schools or with basic aesthetic questions regarding landscape or the exterior shell

15

of school buildings. Yet, as the conversation between the resource team and mayors unfolded, it became clear that the symposium's goal would not be to answer these questions, but rather to reformulate them. Ultimately, the Mayors' Institute introduced mayors to the potential effects of architecture, challenged them to ask new questions with regard to architectural design, and enabled them to reenvision the endless possibilities of school design. As architect Julie Eizenberg eloquently put it: "It is all a question of vision."

The schools that the mayors presented at the symposium fell into two categories: schools that would be newly constructed (Lynn, Massachusetts; Murray City, Utah; San Bernardino, California), and those that would be restored, renovated, or expanded (Wichita, Kansas; Oklahoma City, Oklahoma; Stamford, Connecticut). Each city needed to address a unique set of circumstances and distinct goals. Lynn sought to reinvigorate a stalled downtown neighborhood and to aid this effort through the construction of new schools. Murray City asked for direction in planning a new high school on a busy commercial corridor. Faced with time and budgetary constraints, San Bernardino was grappling with the desire to employ a prototypical school plan while developing some design distinctions to respond to the specific needs of its site. Wichita, a city in which a productive community/government dialogue on school needs has been established, faced the decision of which aging schools to restore, renovate, or replace. Oklahoma City urgently needed to modernize aging facilities, yet hoped to achieve budgetary efficiency through the construction of larger schools. Finally, Stamford sought to imbue a blighted, oft-overlooked inner city neighborhood with a school in which residents could take pride.

As a city in the throes of economic, cultural, and population changes, Lynn has been struggling to define itself. Mayor Patrick J. McManus hoped to create a school that would contribute to the revitalization of the downtown community. This school would serve children living in the several hundred single-family homes that the city recently constructed. Because neighborhood children would walk to school, siting the school in this particular location could help to create a walkable, func-

point for conversation; in contrast, Bob Knight, the mayor of Wichita, presented a process his city had completed based on a dialogue between the citizens and their government. Mayor Knight said, "We engage citizens to find out what they want." One such desire was to establish continuing education classes such as home repair, basic nutrition, Internet training, and parenting skills. The citizens requested access to recreational facilities and programs, as well as school libraries. Mayor Knight explained, "We are maximizing one of our community's greatest assets by opening up the schools to the neighborhood residents before and after the school day ends."

In addition to this conversation with the community, mayor Knight commissioned a facility study on Wichita's schools and determined that the city's aging facilities needed to be updated with regard to energy efficiency, climate control, and programming for technology and community activities. In the end, the Mayor expressed his hope that improvements to urban schools would help make the city's neighborhoods more attractive to residents who might otherwise be tempted to move to the suburbs. With this in mind, the government of the city has determined that renovation and upgrades that allow for flexible programming will be the key to integrating schools into the community fabric.

Panelists encouraged Mayor Knight to take a proactive design approach by suggesting specific architectural possibilities. Architect Sheila Kennedy explained, "When people can't imagine something different, they go back to what they do know because they're afraid that [rather than getting something improved, what they know] would be taken away from them. Civic leaders should work collaboratively with both constituents and architects in order to envision schools." She closed by saying that "one of the best things that design can do is to make us realize that within any given program…there is a wide range of choices that we sometimes don't see. So, that's the kind of x-ray vision that design can offer us."

Like Wichita's, Oklahoma City's schools are aging and in desperate need of repair. Over half of them are 50 years old and all but two are over 30. Kirk Humphreys, mayor of Oklahoma City, explained that because most of the city's schools have not been properly maintained, there is an immediate need for a plan to upgrade and repair existing schools. Efficiency and economy were his primary concerns. While smaller schools are simply more expensive to run, his statistics indicated that they are also more successful at retaining students. This fact put the mayor's own objectives of efficiency and retention at odds. Symposium panelists pushed the issue of school size. They were concerned with the quality of education, noting that smaller school sizes are cited as the second most important factor in creating positive educational outcomes after socioeconomic status. Yet small schools tend to be more costly, so Mayor Humphreys needed compelling reasons to convince his constituents to fund them. Mayor Dannel P. Malloy of Stamford, Connecticut, recommended that Mayor Humphreys go directly to the community to present the educational and social advantages of small schools, including that students remain in a tightly knit educational community for 12 continuous years.

Linking to the conversations begun during the Oklahoma City presentation, Mayor Malloy opened his presentation on Stamford with a discussion of the relationship between architects and politicians. In his view, architects and politicians do not communicate effectively. To counter this tendency, he suggested that architects go beyond the Mayors' Institute to educate the public and politicians about the kinds of architectural issues raised during the symposium. Still, the urban ramifications of school development remained central to the panel's discussion. One participant reminded Mayor Malloy that "When the neighborhood is the weakest, quite often the school is one of the most important institutions and provides the most continuity and anchored quality of any of the other components of the neighborhood including the residential stock, the retail and business opportunities."

The case study Mayor Malloy presented, the Rogers School, is Stamford's only unsuccessful magnet school; the school lags behind in the quality of its facilities. The question Mayor Malloy posed to symposium participants was: Should he tear down Rogers School, or should he recommend renovation? He noted that the school is an important building within its community, and he felt that it would be impossible to rebuild on another site for political reasons. Because the current structure is fraught with architectural problems, Mayor Malloy must reimagine the school, so that people will have a reason to send their children there. Panelists recommended that the mayor consider using the school's architecture to communicate the programmatic changes to the school. In the end, the panel did not offer a definitive decision on whether or not the school should be rebuilt or renovated. But in either instance, the panel agreed that a clear educational vision and the ability to imagine the school in a completely different way would be critical to the success of the project.

"Schools need to function as the centers of our community, and the return when they do is to the whole city," said Chicago architect Carol Ross Barney at the Mayors' Institute public forum. If the question remains one of "vision," the discussions at the sessions began to address how architecture, landscape design, urban design, and innovative programming can combine to reengage communities with their schools. Design discourse is a critical component in the success of schools, as it provides an opportunity for students, teachers, city officials, and their architects to come together around the policies, procedures, and politics that bring schools into being. Design allows people to "see" solutions, to become comfortable with innovation, and to address and enhance the unique qualities of their communities.

- submerge road to make east west pedestrian connection

- explore technology functionality
  component
  first + conduit accessible - style
  of building will follow. Design
  in adaptability for change that are
  use cabinets + interior walls changeable or modular.

- <u>Design</u> the parking lot

  - think about shopping
    mall as organizational
    concept for school.

    anchor
    gym?

  - community life v the strip

    library?
    anchor?

  - make a sociable place.

  - do not under estimate
    grow potential of city

I

Essays

Why Johnny Can't Walk to School

Constance E. Beaumont
Director for State and Local Policy, National Trust for
Historic Preservation

In the middle of an older neighborhood in Spokane, Washington, stands
the Wilson Elementary School, a historic landmark built in 1926.
Renovated in 1999 to meet modern building codes and contemporary
program needs, the Wilson School enters the 21st century with a
decades-old reputation for providing an excellent education well intact.
People love this school. It's small, so students receive lots of personal
attention. Test scores are high compared with those in other schools
around the state. Students can walk safely to school along sidewalks lined
with pleasant trees and well-kept homes. Because of the school's proximi-
ty to the community, it's easy to get to and easy for the school to recruit
volunteers. Neighborhood residents use the school for civic and other
activities in the evenings.

The school is a handsome building that fits in well with the neighborhood. It's not surrounded by parking, but comes up close to the street.
Visually and historically, the school is an anchor. Its presence on
Spokane's South Hill is one of the main reasons people move into—and
stay in—this neighborhood. The school enhances property values and
stabilizes an older part of the city. Having served four generations of students, the Wilson School represents an important part of Spokane's
history. In short, Wilson is a small, community-centered school that edu-
cates kids while bringing a whole neighborhood together. It's exactly the

A "sprawl school" on a
remote site in South
Carolina.

27

The Franklin High School in Seattle was built in 1912 but renovated to meet state-of-the-art standards in 1990.

kind of school that many educators and parents across the country seek to replicate today.

But if you tried to build or renovate a school like Wilson today, you could not do so in many places. That's because Wilson sits on just two acres of land, a small site that would be considered "substandard" by most school districts. A combination of national guidelines, state policies, and advice handed out by private consultants often makes it difficult to retain and renovate—or even build new—small, community-centered schools like Wilson.

Having heard from parents, civic leaders, and others around the country about barriers to preserving—or creating—schools akin to the Wilson School, the National Trust for Historic Preservation decided to examine public policies affecting school construction and renovation. How do policies affect the size and location of schools and community interaction? Do funding biases work against the proper maintenance and modernization of older schools? These were among the questions asked during a study that culminated with the release of a report, *Why Johnny Can't Walk to School*, in November 2000. This report provides educators, community leaders, architects, and other interested parties with effective strategies for preserving schools as neighborhood anchors and significant community landmarks.[1]

28

Major Study Findings

Acreage Standards

Acreage standards top the list of policy barriers to preserving and renovating historic schools—and to building well-designed new schools—in
older neighborhoods. Many jurisdictions follow national model guidelines
that recommend one acre of land for every 100 students, plus an
additional 10 acres for an elementary school, 20 acres for a middle school,
and 30 acres for a high school.

The problem with these standards is that they often leave school
districts with one of two bad choices:

- Destroy perfectly good homes near the school to meet the acreage
  standards. In Mansfield, Ohio, the school district recently demolished almost 60 homes to clear a 50-acre site for a new high
  school. People wanted a school in the neighborhood, but in order
  to provide one, the neighborhood was destroyed.

- Find a large open space—often a working farm—and build a
  "sprawl school" in the middle of nowhere. In Two Rivers,
  Wisconsin, the school district recently purchased almost 80 acres
  of farmland for a new school. Most of this land is for parking and
  a massive sports complex; the school itself will occupy only a small
  portion of the site. Meanwhile, Two Rivers is closing an in-town
  school that had served an older neighborhood for decades.

These siting decisions can create transportation problems. When schools
are located on isolated sites and too far away for students to walk to, they
are almost always engulfed by acres of parking. Even when older schools
must be torn down, current standards make it hard to replace them with
new schools on the same site in built-up, close-knit neighborhoods with
no room to expand. Although many large cities have managed to obtain
waivers from the acreage requirements, mid-size and smaller cities gener-
ally have not, even though the preservation of neighborhood anchors
such as schools is as important to smaller communities as to big ones.

Biases in State Funding Formulas

State funding formulas are another major policy problem, for they often discriminate unreasonably against the renovation of existing schools, even when that option makes good sense for economic and educational reasons. An example of such a bias is Ohio's "two-thirds rule," which says if the cost of renovating an older school exceeds 66 percent of the cost of a new school, the state will not help pay for the project. The numbers vary from state to state: Virginia has a 50 percent rule; Minnesota has a 60 percent rule. Although waivers are sometimes granted, the burden of justifying them falls on the community.

The problem with using these arbitrary percentage rules is that they trivialize the relationship between older schools and their neighborhoods and prevent full cost analyses. They ignore many costs tied to new construction—such as the cost of extending water and sewer lines, building new roads, buying land, or demolishing a school taken out of service. If these costs were considered, renovation projects might meet the percentage rule more easily. Why *not* renovate schools when doing so produces state-of-the-art results *and* saves money?

Farmland outside Granville, Ohio. Nearby, a new school under construction on 179 acres (inset). Some local residents had argued in favor of building the school on a smaller site closer to existing neighborhoods.

The Kirk Middle School in East Cleveland, Ohio, one of the city's most important landmarks, was effectively condemned by the state's "two-thirds rule." Had the cost of demolishing Kirk been considered, the renovation project would have passed the rule.

Planning Conflicts

In many jurisdictions, local land-use and school-facility planning are completely disconnected, even though the construction of new schools in certain areas can dramatically change a town's future growth patterns. Building a school on farmland can force a town to speed up the construction of new roads, water mains, and sewer lines in places that might otherwise stay rural. At the same time, resources consumed for new-school construction in outlying areas can drain the budgets needed to maintain and renovate existing schools in town. As W. Cecil Steward, dean emeritus of the University of Nebraska's College of Architecture, has written: "The public school system…is the most influential planning entity, either public or private, promoting the…sprawl pattern of American cities." He describes some public school systems as "advance scouts for urban sprawl."[2] An example is East Bradford Township in Pennsylvania, where the school district condemned 100 acres of farmland slated for protection by the local land-use plan. At the same time, the school district announced the closing of an in-town school, which stands exactly where local residents said they wanted civic buildings. Fortunately, this decision was reversed.

Solutions

The National Trust for Historic Preservation's report suggests two general approaches to finding solutions. First, review and reform well-intentioned policies that are producing unintended results. Maryland, Pennsylvania, Maine, and California are states that have changed their rules regarding the renovation of older school buildings or required school boards and planning agencies to share their plans for new or expanded school facilities. Second, examine how school boards can successfully maintain and bring older schools up to 21st-century educational standards. Boise, Idaho; Manitowoc, Wisconsin; Spokane, Washington; and Columbia, South Carolina, have all invested funds to renovate and expand schools on sites that allow students to walk to school and participate in after-school jobs and activities.

Clearly, older schools can be, and have been, adapted to meet today's safety and educational program needs. And school officials can reach agreements with city parks, nearby churches and public transit and other agencies to share playing fields, parking spaces, and transportation services.

Missions and Values

Although the mission of educators is not historic preservation, they share an interest with preservationists in strong neighborhoods, the kind that provide a good support system for students during after-school hours. They also share an interest in smaller, community-centered schools, albeit for different reasons. Educators like these kinds of schools because they give students the personal attention they need. Preservationists like them because they fit gracefully into, and strengthen, older neighborhoods. When educators choose to preserve and update historic schools, they often simultaneously strengthen a neighborhood's identity and sense of community. Preserving and upgrading historic schools or creating new, well-designed schools in close-knit, walkable neighborhoods—like the one surrounding Spokane's Wilson School—offers many benefits to children. Enabling students to walk or bike to school gives them greater independence and promotes healthy forms of physical fitness.

Schools teach values as well as academic skills. Environmental stewardship is one such value. The irony of teaching kids to recycle paper and cans while abandoning older buildings is captured by a parent trying to save his daughter's school: "They have recycling bins in the cafeteria, and yet they were planning to cart the whole school off to the landfill."[3]

As Lakis Polycarpou, a young graduate of Columbine High School, points out, we have choices:

> Of course we will always need some new schools. But we have a choice in how we build them. Will they carry a sense of permanence, dignity, respect for education and the public life? Or will they be interchangeable and disposable? Will they be built as the center of a community—an anchor for civic life—or will they be put on the outskirts of town as magnets for sprawl?[4]

The National Trust for Historic Preservation believes that public policies should make it easier for communities to preserve and renovate historic neighborhood schools when it is feasible to adapt them for contemporary educational programs. When it is not, the system should make it easier to build well-designed new schools *in the same neighborhood* without destroying nearby homes. The rules should not compel communities to shoehorn "cornfield architecture" into urban settings or to replace existing schools with sprawl schools on remote sites. As Mr. Polycarpou adds: "The choice is not between the old and the new—it is between the dignified and the undistinguished, the enduring and the disposable. It is a choice between thoughtless replication of sprawl and the conscious decision to invest in civic life."[5]

Lessons from the Chicago Public Schools Design Competition

Cindy S. Moelis with Beth Valukas
Business and Professional People for the Public Interest

> Most city schools are too big, and anonymity among students is
> a pervasive problem....Overcoming anonymity—creating a set-
> ting in which every student is known personally by an adult—is
> one of the most compelling obligations urban schools confront.
> —*Carnegie Foundation for the*
> *Advancement of Teaching*, 1988

p. 34:
Architect Julie Eizenberg presents the winning design for the North Side site.

Judging the competition entries.

Above:
Larry Gorski speaking at the Chicago Public Schools Design Competition press conference, August 2000. As the director of the Mayor's Office for People with Disabilities, the late Larry Gorski helped form Chicago's mission to become the most accessible city in the nation.

Those concerned with public education know that it is not just how we teach but also the buildings that we teach in that nourish the great potential of students. Can we combine the best design ideas that architects have to offer, while answering the creative dreams of students and teachers? One challenge for government, education, and community leaders is to define the form, scale, and aesthetics of the 21st-century public school. To meet this challenge, it is imperative to bring educators, architects, and community members to the table to discuss the solution. Collaboration "creates real dialogue between architects and educators about how a building can help achieve a pedagogical goal."[1] The Chicago Public Schools Design Competition is a model for such collaboration. By culti-vating a high level of engaged, active community input in the design of schools, the final architectural solutions demonstrated that urban school architecture can be at once intimate, innovative, practical, and affordable, and, as a result, inspire school systems to be more thoughtful and intentional about new school design.

In the fall of 1999, representatives from Business and Professional People for the Public Interest (BPI), Leadership for Quality Education (LQE) (both Chicago organizations that advocate more intimate learning environments), and Mayor Richard M. Daley's Office for People with Disabilities came together.[2] Together, the group ("the sponsors") was looking for creative and feasible ways to design innovative new school buildings that nurture student potential and reflect the communities in which they reside. Research demonstrates that students thrive in smaller learning environments that foster interaction and maximize interaction with the greater community.[3] Chicago Public Schools (CPS) have embraced the development of smaller schools since 1995. At the time of the Chicago Public Schools Design Competition, the rate of new school construction in the United States had reached a peak, surpassing the efforts of every previous generation in history. In 2000, over $21 billion was spent on schools nationwide, with nearly half of those dollars spent on over 700 new school buildings.

It was in the context of this unprecedented boom in new school construction and renovation that the sponsors began to discuss a school design competition to combine the best contemporary ideas in education reform and design for state-of-the-art educational environments. At the start of the competition there were approximately 100 small schools, including 13 charter schools, in Chicago.[4] Yet, CPS had not incorporated small school educational philosophy into their design process for new school prototype construction. Since its beginning in 1996, the Chicago Public Schools Capital Improvement Program has committed more than $2.6 billion towards improving CPS facilities.

The competition was based on a vision that schools should complement their neighborhood communities: that small schools can flourish, even in buildings serving 800 to 900 students; that school buildings should be accessible to all; that innovative, sustainable, and environmentally sensitive designs are possible within the constraints of a public budget. The competition focused on two separate sites, one each on the city's North and South

Sides. CPS officials promised to build the winning design for each site.[5] Each new school would accommodate students from two existing schools for an integrated population of 800 disabled and non-disabled students.

A primary objective of the competition was to engage the entire school community in the design process. Recognizing that schools are at the heart of a community, the competition's sponsors sought to create an approach that would capture input from those individuals and groups that best understood the needs of schools: the people who work, learn, and live in and around them. A steering committee comprising developers, financiers, architects, academics, advocates, educators, and funders was formed to guide the process.[6] The competition was designed as a two-stage process; the first stage featured both "invited" and "open" components. The "invited" component began with a Request for Proposals issued in July 2000 to a national group of architects. Four of these firms were chosen by a panel of architects, educators, and sponsor-representatives to advance to the second round.[7] The four "invited" architects were KoningEizenberg Architecture (Santa Monica), Mack Scogin Merrill Elam Architects (Atlanta), Smith-Miller + Hawkinson Architects (New York), and Ross Barney + Jankowski (Chicago). An open call, which was judged by a jury of national architects and community representatives,[8] was made in August 2000 inviting all architects and architecture students from around the world to submit designs and to compete for the four remaining "open" spaces in the competition.[9]

Once the eight finalists were identified, in January 2001, the second round began: an interactive community learning process before the completion of final designs, engaging the school community and the architectural firms in dialogues about architecture and education. Each of the new schools was to offer comprehensive programs that serve developmentally delayed, physically disabled, or otherwise health-impaired children. Architects and educators would need to address questions about the integration of these programs and the implications for both special facilities and classroom activities. In addition, three of the competition's central tenets—small schools, sustainability, and universal design—were new, unfamiliar concepts to the communities and, in some cases, the architects involved in the competition. The interactive participation of school and neighborhood communities was critical in the development of designs that were sensitive to the individual character of each neighborhood setting.

From the beginning, the sponsors solicited community input through school visits, task forces, community forums, and informal meetings, many of which directly involved the competition finalists. Hundreds of community members and architects turned out for these events. Undoubtedly, this approach was instrumental in the creation of strong and innovative designs that actively responded to the unique needs of the local communities. These events also served as catalysts for a greater awareness of sustainable and universal design principles within the larger Chicago architectural community.

The first forum introduced the school communities to the competition's main tenets.[10] The goal of a universal design school is to maximize functionality for all users while maintaining high architectural standards. This community forum also provided an opportunity to introduce small school philosophies and benefits to program participants. The architects were asked to produce designs that could easily facilitate the schools' organization into several small schools-within-schools. Given economies of scale and public building budgets, large urban schools broken into smaller units with shared central facilities are often the most realistic way to achieve intimate learning environments. Later forums enabled more direct interaction between the architects and the schools' constituents. At one forum, advisory panels from the four schools, local historians, and experts in the fields of green design, universal design, and small schools publicly discussed the merits of each design.

The architects who participated in this process felt that community feedback both changed their design ideas for the competition and impacted how they would conceive future work. Laurie Hawkinson of Smith-Miller + Hawkinson commented: "There are things we learned at the community forums—particularly about universal design—that changed us as architects, that changed the way we think about accessibility and that we will bring to our future projects." Architects learned

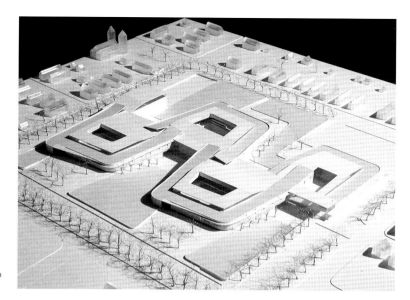

Marble · Fairbanks Architects' winning design for the South Side site.

KoningEizenberg Architecture's winning design for the North Side site.

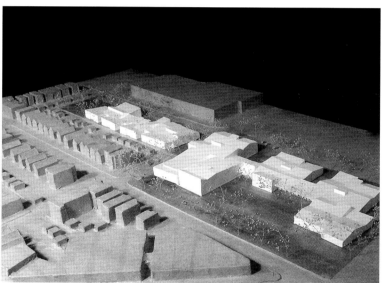

Principal Rochelle Riddick
meets with architects at
the Davis Developmental
Center.

Site visit to the Langston
Hughes School.

important applications for these new ideas to be integrated into their
methods of presentation and their general practice.

Community input prompted a range of changes to the original
designs, from the addition of a community garden to energy-saving
modifications. One winning team, Marble · Fairbanks Architects (New
York), recognized that it would be important for the long-term flexibility
and sustainability of the small schools to have direct connections with
each other. Throughout the competition, it became clear that the intense
level of community participation resulted in stronger, more responsive
designs. The competition and numerous stages of discussion and revision
encouraged an inclusive approach to the designs. Architects, school
administrators, teachers, students, and parents collaborated to develop
designs responsive to the needs of the school communities and the cultures of each neighborhood. Each group that participated in the
competition had a unique perspective to contribute, and the public
process ensured community impact on the final submissions. The superb
winning designs, submitted by Marble · Fairbanks Architects and
KoningEizenberg Architecture, are convincing evidence that a collaborative, community-focused process can produce stronger design results.
The two designs have received national recognition and numerous architectural awards.[11]

Conclusion

> We felt, through the community process and the open nature of the competition, that we really came to view the other finalists as collaborators—not as competitors. And that is the future—not to protect ideas, but to put them out there to grow organically.
>
> —Scott Marble
> *Marble · Fairbanks Architects*

Beyond building two new schools for Chicago, the competition's sponsors sought to create a process that could serve as a model for other architects, educators, and community activists interested in building schools. The community process was an integral part of creating these innovative designs. Chicago Public Schools have promised to begin building the schools by the year 2004. Once built, the schools will truly be community centers, reflective of the neighborhoods in which they exist. The buildings themselves will help inspire and engage the people living in the community, while the teaching will enlighten those inside. Yet the true impact of the competition goes well beyond these two buildings. The work of the architects, who partnered with participating communities, sets a new standard for the community-based planning process for building schools. The competition triggered interest and discourse in the architecture community about the need to bring different voices into the creative process and how to build schools that support educational needs of the 21st century. The competition generated an enormous body of learning on blending educational and design innovation, while creating excitement nationally about the possibilities for public school architecture. Business and Professional People for the Public Interest will capture the lessons learned and highlight the innovative designs created for the competition in a publication to be released in the fall of 2002.[12] It is clear that the competition and the designs produced can serve as models for schools, communities, architects, policymakers, and others committed to thoughtful school design in the United States.

Something from "Nothing": Information Infrastructure in School Design

Sheila Kennedy
Kennedy & Violich Architecture

Introduction

Infrastructure in American culture is normally thought to be invisible. Because infrastructure is useful, it is not understood as part of the realm of design. Yet infrastructure is clearly operative—it affects the organization of space and program activities. In school design, we cannot afford to continue the distinction between operation and aesthetic experience. The scarcity of resources to build and repair schools is motivation on one hand, and on the other is the need to prepare students to be continual learners in a culture increasingly dominated by technology.

This essay describes an alternative approach to the design of elementary schools, one where infrastructure and architecture are integrated to transform school buildings and produce new kinds of classrooms, curricular opportunities, and community resources. This approach calls for architects, school boards, and teachers to look with fresh eyes at existing and new forms of infrastructure to see how these operative elements can support the intellectual and public life of the school community. The imagination of a child at play is the inspiration that can transform objects

Jackson School and Brighton Public Plaza, Boston, Massachusetts

Classroom for the study of public housing, Techwood Housing, Atlanta, Georgia

43

by seeing beyond things as they are. A cardboard box can be anything; what is needed is the vision to create something from what may appear to be "nothing."

A Fresh Approach to School Design

School design in the United States has become highly conventional, due in part to well-intentioned building codes and standardized specification guidelines for materials and building systems. These legal and perform-ance standards were created for the public good, however in practice they tend to produce an unchallenged and unnecessary adherence to school building typologies—an institutionalized organization of architecture. This promotes the reason of habit—"it's always been done this way"—regardless of whether these conventions are actually better for the experi-ence of students, teachers or parents. As a building typology, the American school is an institution ripe for change.

The creative stance of "something from nothing" is supported by three interlocking arguments:

- *The ethical argument* calls for making the best creative use of resources in an era of reduced funding for public schools.
- *The entrepreneurial argument* calls for maximizing the pragmatic value of design by creating value in new construction and renova-tion.
- *The curricular argument* calls for design as a vehicle for educational reform and community-oriented change for those who are willing to challenge conventions.

Information Infrastructure: More than "Wires"

The physical form of a city is shaped by its urban infrastructure. Our office has developed a design strategy that engages the physical design opportunities provided by freeways, housing projects, parks, and roadways to create public space for teaching and learning. The Interim Bridges Project takes advantage of an archeological excavation at a central artery site in Boston slated to become a new underground roadway. The design of a covered structure, funded by a grant from the NEA, served as a public teaching platform for the history of the city. At Techwood Housing in Atlanta, an abandoned apartment was transformed into a classroom for the Fowler Elementary School. Children saw historic film clips and read articles from 50 years ago to better understand their heritage as inhabitants of the nation's first public housing project. In a design for the Jackson School in Boston, Massachusetts, a series of small, unusable traffic islands were collected and transformed into a significant new public outdoor plaza for the school. Similar principles can be applied to institutions for higher education, such as our projects for a new building for the School of the Art Institute of Chicago and the New Graduate Center for the Rhode Island School of Design.

A school's program and its building form are shaped by the organization of information infrastructure. The miniaturization and interconnectivity of contemporary technology create a different set of conditions for school design. The physical world has not been "replaced" by the digital world, as was once initially predicted. Instead, we are discovering that the digital world is increasingly absorbed into and merged with the physical world. Cellphones, pagers, and digital toys and games are a few examples of the many very sophisticated kinds of interfaces that already exist in the daily world of children and their families. The materials of the physical world and these everyday realities of information-based infrastructure are increasingly interwoven.

The traditional relationship between physical scale and presence in architecture changes when information infrastructure is overlaid onto building infrastructure. Access to power, location of data ports, types of networks and display systems, seating, lighting, and scales of school space directly affect learning and teaching practices. The expression "wiring" the classroom is misleading. Information infrastructure is more than just "wires"; it is programmatic and spatial. As an integral part of school design, the implementation of digital infrastructure can act as a catalyst to improve the spatial organization of schools and the ways in which classrooms and classroom furniture are designed and used.

The Digital Diaspora: Integrating Traditional and Digital Teaching Resources

The Canton Elementary School in Canton, Ohio, and the Shady Hill Library in Cambridge, Massachusetts, projects designed by Kennedy & Violich Architecture, share two important design principles. The first design principle recognizes that digital infrastructure can be successfully integrated into traditional forms of building infrastructure. By overlaying or nesting information infrastructure into the circulation pathways of existing school typologies, better common spaces with multiple uses are created for traditionally underused spaces such as corridors, stairways, social areas, and lobbies. Funding for new or upgraded information infrastructure can help to trigger improvements for a school's physical design.

The second design principle moves away from the conventional appliance approach to computers. The appliance approach doesn't acknowledge the way digital learning is inscribed into the space of the classroom, changing the manner in which children acquire information, relate to their teachers and peers, and understand relationships *between* the classes in their curriculum.

We would find it laughable today to retreat into an isolated "electricity room" to use artificial lights and power outlets. But this segregated approach happens when school design calls for a "computer room." Architects and curriculum developers need to work together to reconsider where computers are located and how and when they are used. A digital "diaspora" serves to strengthen curriculum relationships as it disperses learning resources into alternate sites such as a library, theater or performance spaces, and specialty classrooms such as art, music, and science.

An integrated approach is recommended whenever possible, especially in program development for new school construction. School

Canton Elementary School,
Canton, Ohio

Satellite space

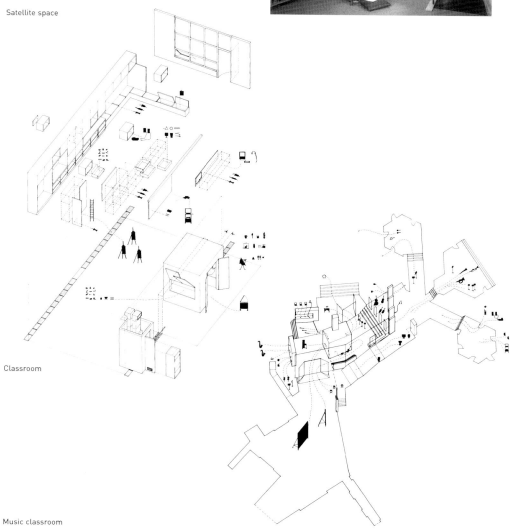

Classroom

Music classroom

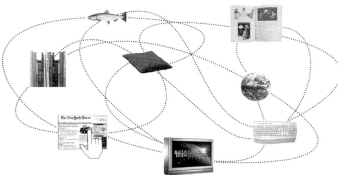

Shady Hill Library,
Cambridge, Massachusetts

Interactive knowledge

Sitting area

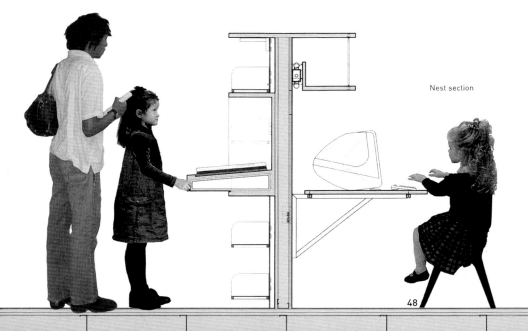

Nest section

48

design is often treated as if building types were "given" forms. Architects, school boards, and building committees must ask how schools can take best advantage of information infrastructure within the larger context of other emerging building technologies. Electrical power requirements can be supplemented by solar- and wind-generated energy sources. Energy-efficient lighting, heating, cooling, and ventilation systems are currently available and can be designed with significant short- and long-term cost savings. In-cycling programs can be implemented within existing schools, and school construction materials need to be reconsidered at the state and federal levels.

The first generation of contemporary materials, such as hard plastics and laminate veneers, once specified for hygienic reasons, do not wear well in practice. An expanding palette of sustainable materials, often the byproducts of other material manufacturing processes, can be harvested and introduced in school design. These recycled materials meet necessary criteria for maintenance and durability. A rich learning environment can be created from these affordable materials. As digital information becomes ubiquitous, materials can provide an enhanced tactile stimulus in the classroom. School design can respect the sophistication of children and their familiarity with the digital world. The GUI or graphic user interface—looking at a screen—is a limited mode of interaction, only a bit less passive than watching television. The next generation of information infrastructure will be characterized by more portable computation devices children will use in conjunction with systems of display and interaction embedded into the material surfaces of the classroom.

Information is not the same as knowledge. Information infrastructure places new importance on the design of the school's physical environment as a means of producing knowledge from information. The architecture of schools (as well as homes and workplaces) must support children as they learn how to make critical assessments, test assumptions, correlate and synthesize information, and check sources. Architects must learn how to invent flexibly scaled teaching and learning spaces to respond to needs for collaborative, team, and individual study areas for children of different ages and levels of learning. Discussion in small or larger group settings will coexist with spaces for analyzing, editing, and presenting information by working with text, images, and media. One of the primary tasks for architecture is to create an environment for these cognitive activities: a thinking space, or more accurately, a space where people are able to discuss, analyze, and think creatively to produce knowledge about a problem at hand. Wireless access to information offers a new freedom of ergonomics and the possibility to design furniture and architectural elements with appropriate lighting, heating, and cooling systems to support a renewed humanism in school design.

Something from "Nothing"

The diversity of urban experience produces a need for "commonness" and community gathering space. In a time where there is not a consensus about how our public institutions should look, when there is not a singular demographic profile for the American "public," the infrastructure of schools as civic institutions is one of our country's most significant common denominators. As a shared public resource, it makes sense for information infrastructure in school design to function as a multipurpose learning platform, usable by many members of the community. The community's investment is more rapidly amortized if schools can be designed so that selected areas can function on weekends and evenings. Schools can serve many constituents by engaging digital infrastructure to provide adult education, instruction in English as a second language, research opportunities, and vocational instruction. These schools require a new spatial freedom in their design. By designing built-in versatility in their typology, schools may cross over to provide some functions of a social center, public library, town hall, or theater.

The need to provide information infrastructure is not merely an opportunity to "upgrade" the status quo. Instead, it offers a significant opportunity for architectural invention and curricular change. The physical and digital infrastructures of school buildings are key links between architecture and curriculum.

The seemingly prosaic problems of how to "wire" schools are in fact critical strategic design issues. A design process that engages the strategic, spatial implications of infrastructure offers a remarkable opportunity to rethink the architectural organization of schools, and the character of a school's public spaces and classrooms. The time children spend in school and after-school programs is increasing, as many families have two working parents. Now more than ever, the issue is how to redefine conventional assumptions about school design and create alternative visions for what schools can be. An integrated, flexible, and public design is "something" that can be created from the spatial, substantial "nothing" of information infrastructure.

WELL I LIKE THE SEELing
IN Mi CEAS rom SAM

GRAYSON

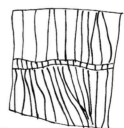

I like that the bridge is really
strong to walk on and I like
how it is made.

prioritize their concerns. We presented several schemes for them to review, which allowed the community to see various ideas, making them more real and leading to a more informed decision.

This process does require the architect to be flexible and to acknowledge that people will change their minds, but designing is a creative and iterative process in which intention can only be evaluated through the product. By sharing knowledge, we build trust and consensus with our clients. At the school, our early visualization (or first draft) demonstrated that moving the front office upstairs would allow us to maximize the playground area. But the parents and faculty had to become comfortable with a nonconventional solution (a buzzer/keypad to control the entry gate) in exchange for retaining the relaxed personality of the original building.

This design process mirrors the progressive educational methods used at PS#1, which are intended to help children learn how to learn and to take an active role in the learning process. The environment itself should hold information about the world for them to discover or for educators to use to illustrate ideas. The design of PS#1 also responds to these ideals. Its roof—a hyperbolic paraboloid structure—is explicitly shown, and kids can trace how a column holds up a beam, and a beam, a roof. Texture is celebrated. The movement of light is valued, and all rooms are day-lit and cross-ventilated. Each classroom has its own outdoor space. Subscribing to ecological values is much more meaningful for children if they see the environment valued in their daily life. Nothing is designed as a "throwaway." With mild weather, covered outside space provides circulation and is an opportunity for social interaction. It is made up of stopping places with attention to the sequence of views and the color and texture of floor and wall surfaces. Not surprisingly, the bridge that safely links the site across the alley is one of the children's favorite places because it provides a space from which they can view their surroundings.

Traditionally, what people think of as a playground appropriate for children is a large paved space to run around, a sports field, and a play structure. Kids need more than that. They need a variety of spaces for improvised play where they can use their minds creatively and work out social relationships. Play is a form of learning. The traditional design of schools undervalues the legitimacy of play and isolates inside classroom space and work from outdoor space and play. From a kid's point of view, what message are we sending? That knowledge is serious and only found in one setting, and that play, like the outdoor space typically provided for it, is of little meaning. Ideally, school environments should value both work and play, inside and outside, suggesting a more holistic framework for learning and life.

The school was finished three years ago and is thriving. Like most schools, it was built on a tight budget, but from what I hear as a parent at the school other parents and teachers find it an inspiring, supportive environment; it met their expectations and more as a result of the collaborative design process. The students of PS#1 have demonstrated that they understand the principles behind the creation of their school. About a year after construction was finished, at "moving up day," my younger son insisted that we not show up late for the events. The school presented us with a package of 165 drawings and notes. Each child had drawn and written something about the school that was interesting to them. The students drew the roof trusses; they meticulously detailed the assembly of the bridge. Some children favored the new equipment, like the 10-year-old who drew the new computers. Other children drew the stairs and the concrete wall that supports them, noting the pattern of the concrete lug holes left by the formwork and the adjacent railing with its alternating slat design. The students noticed patterns, structures, color, and spaces. They wrote about the view of trees and what they liked to do in different spaces. These drawings and notes confirmed that children understand their environment. If they notice their buildings and the nature in their play spaces, it is not a leap to suggest that they can understand their city. Designing from principles that bring together student experience with environmental engagement does make a difference, and if it doesn't cost more, surely it is well worth the risk. Maybe it isn't even a risk, but an obligation.

The school in its site,
Avery's view

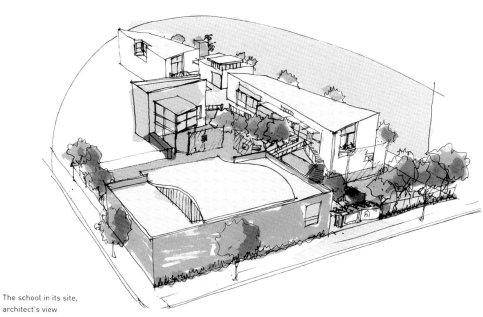

The school in its site,
architect's view

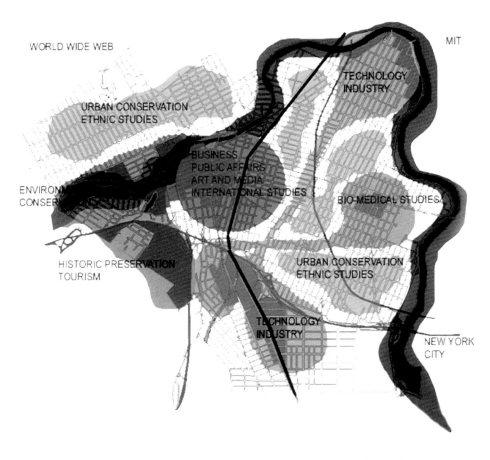

WORLD WIDE WEB

MIT

URBAN CONSERVATION
ETHNIC STUDIES

TECHNOLOGY
INDUSTRY

BUSINESS
PUBLIC AFFAIRS
ART AND MEDIA
INTERNATIONAL STUDIES

BIO-MEDICAL STUDIES

ENVIRON
CONSER

HISTORIC PRESERVATION
TOURISM

URBAN CONSERVATION
ETHNIC STUDIES

TECHNOLOGY
INDUSTRY

NEW YORK
CITY

Paterson lesson plan

60

The City of Learning: Schools as Agents for Urban Revitalization

Roy Strickland
Taubman College of Architecture and Urban Planning,
University of Michigan

Introduction

Over the next decade, the United States will spend between $200 billion and $400 billion on new and renovated schools. For many communities, shares in this investment represent the largest capital expenditure in recent history—an extraordinary opportunity to enhance not just the delivery of education but the quality of community life. With it, architects, planners, educators, and developers may combine efforts to revitalize towns and cities as they expand educational opportunity, one of 21st-century America's greatest challenges. The approach described in this essay recommends collaboration among these groups as they define school construction strategies in their local communities.

City of Learning™ (COL) is a strategy for combining school and urban design and development. COL embraces educators' arguments that healthy neighborhoods support successful learning and make school design and programming holistic by looking beyond the school building to the school setting at the neighborhood, town, and city scales. By coordinating school projects with housing, economic development, and job-training initiatives, COL identifies schools as a potent new force in urban revitalization as it expands pre-K–12 educational options.

Impetus

COL is the outgrowth of the New American School Design Project (NASDP) that I founded in 1993 at the MIT School of Architecture and Planning. I have carried this program to the University of Michigan, where I now direct the Master of Urban Design Program at the Taubman College of Architecture and Urban Planning. NASDP's original objective was the correlation of architectural design with the discussion of American public school reform. From Berkeley, California, to Washington, D.C., public school students, teachers, parents, and administrators emphasized that the school building was but one factor among many in successful learning environments. Looking beyond the walls of the school building, they recognized that the social, physical, and economic character of surrounding neighborhoods played important roles in a school's performance and quality of life.[1] This insight is reinforced by educational literature from John Dewey to Howard Gardner in which schools are proposed as parts of larger systems of resources including museums, parks, places of work, and—critically—the home.[2] In response, NASDP expanded its focus from the school building to the school setting, or the blocks, neighborhoods, towns, and cities surrounding school sites where resources such as those identified by Dewey and Gardner could be integrated with school programming or be designed and built to support school programs as they provided resources to the larger community.

Principles

COL is built on the premise that teachers and learners can contribute to community life, and community resources can contribute to learning. It reflects educational reform movements such as small schools, pilot schools, and public/private partnerships; technology's influence on learning, school administration, and spatial design; and the social capital and economic power of school students, teachers, and staff. Its principles are:

1. *Integrate COL stakeholders—teachers, students, administrators, parents, and civic and business leaders—into the planning process.* As COL seeks synergies between schools and communities, school planning should encourage the participation of all members of the community.

2. *Break out of the "big box" school.* Big schools require large sites and/or neighborhood displacement, while their self-containment isolates them from communities. Small schools sharing centrally located resource facilities minimize displacement and make learning accessible to members of the community.

3. *Coordinate school projects as part of a strategic plan.* School projects can represent the largest capital investments in neighborhoods and towns, yet they are often planned individually, thus separating schools and their communities.

4. *Inventory learning opportunities in neighborhoods and towns and construct a "lesson plan" derived from local resources.* From Dewey to Gardner, educators advocate "learning by doing." Resources such as cultural institutions, libraries, hospitals, industry, commerce, etc., should be tied into school planning as supplements to school facilities and their programs through internships, mentoring, and work-study programs.

5. *Inventory neighborhood and town sites and buildings as opportunities for various kinds of learning and recreation facilities.* Follow the lead of private and charter schools in their inventive reuse of buildings such as former houses, commercial buildings, clubs, and factories. Consider using public parks and libraries and institutions such as YMCAs and YWCAs and Boys and Girls Clubs to reduce the size and cost of school projects.

6. *Where possible, mix uses at school sites.* Compatible uses such as commercial, professional, and cultural activities can help support educational programs with internships, mentoring, and work-study opportunities, while education-related businesses can test products and help staff development.

7. *Coordinate agencies, programs, and funding sources that can contribute to school projects.* Educational dollars should be leveraged with federal, state, and local dollars as part of strategic planning. Housing, community development, transportation funds, etc., can help integrate school projects with local planning and development goals.

8. *Consider the private sector in delivering learning facilities and services.* Leasing, lease-to-buy, turnkey, and condominium arrangements with the private sector open opportunities for new forms of learning facilities as they provide potential development and tax revenues for localities.

9. *Include learning space in buildings of all types.* As schools share space with other users, other building types such as office buildings, hotels, hospitals, or museums should be designed to include flexible learning space in order to offer alternative educational and employment opportunities for students.

10. *Use technology to support COL.* Technology can tie together dispersed learning facilities, serve as a monitoring and management tool, and reduce facility duplication by linking common resources and staff.

COL Applied: Union City, Paterson, and Trenton

In 1998, the New Jersey State Supreme Court handed down its *Abbott v. Burke* ruling, upholding the state's constitutional guarantee of equal access to education after a New Jersey resident successfully argued hardship as the result of inferior urban public school education. In response, New Jersey plans to spend $12 billion on school capital projects over the

COL team member
LaTonya Green and
Metro-Paterson Academy
for Communications &
Technology students

Paterson Parkland
Corridor

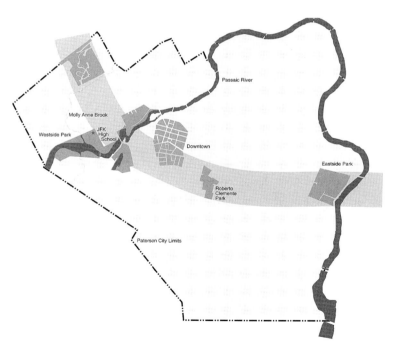

Concept Diagrams
Reuse of Empty Buildings
Downtown Paterson

Commercial
Education
Residential

5-9 Colt Street   126 Market Street

Converted office buildings,
downtown Paterson

Paterson neighborhoods
for learning connections

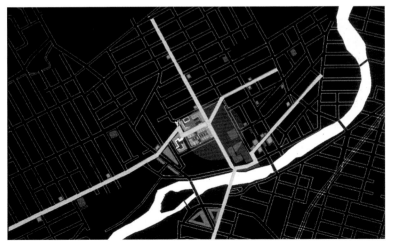

next 10 years to help urban school districts achieve parity with those in more affluent suburban areas. The focus of much of this expenditure will be 28 "Abbott" school districts serving the state's older cities. Three of these districts—Union City, Paterson, and Trenton—are currently engaged in COL plans for projects totaling approximately $1.3 billion.[3] Many postindustrial cities such as these suffer deficits in housing, schools, and employment in the wake of middle-class flight to the suburbs. For these and similar New Jersey towns, the school-building initiative represents an opportunity for social and economic stabilization and growth.

In Union City, a town of 70,000 people, the school system is distributing the program for a 1,200-seat pre-K–8 school across three sites within a five-minute walking radius. Rather than build a single large school in the town's only major park (the school system's original plan), planners adapted COL principles to recapture two empty historic buildings nearby, erect a smaller building on the original site, and maintain as much open space as possible for the use of the entire town and school system. The three buildings will be linked by street and landscape improvements that will enhance and give visual coherence to a residential neighborhood and will share resources such as a library and technology/media-arts center with other nearby schools.

In Paterson, a city of 170,000 people, the school system is using COL principles to plan its program for "Innovative Academies" in residential neighborhoods and the city's downtown. Like Union City, Paterson has restricted open space. There are, however, many underutilized buildings in the city, including commercial space at the center of town. Since the fall of 1999, Paterson has opened several academies, including three in downtown. There the city plans to locate additional academies as part of a "downtown campus" where students will share classrooms and resources in converted commercial and institutional space. One of these academies, located in the upper floor of a former retail mall on the city's main shopping street, focuses on architecture and urban planning for the city, including new school projects, and makes students active agents in the city's renewal. Another, located in a former church, focuses on the performing arts, opening its doors for concerts that make students contributors to the town's cultural life. A third, opened in an old office building in cooperation with a local school of education, focuses on careers in teaching and will, in turn, help the school system replenish itself with teachers from the community. Combined with a nearby community college, nearly 6,000 people involved in teaching and learning will eventually inhabit the downtown area, providing a positive environment for compatible private development such as retail and entertainment facilities.

In Trenton, New Jersey's capital, the state's planning office has awarded a smart-growth grant to the municipal government and school system to explore opportunities for linking the design of new schools with community development and housing. Four school sites are currently under study, each in widely differing urban conditions: a low-income residential community; a historic industrial complex; a downtown lot adjacent to a community college and the main branch of the public library; and an abandoned block. As these schools are shaped to address the needs and opportunities of their neighborhoods, they will be programmed and planned as an arc of facilities related to each other and to Trenton's centers of government, communications, tourism, and culture.

Conclusion

As COL work proceeds, its New Jersey projects are beginning to display results. In Union City, the school system is currently renovating an abandoned building as part of its planned cluster of school facilities and has added another component, a high school careers program in the first two floors of a new affordable housing project. In Paterson, the school system has already opened several academies according to COL principles. In the downtown area, merchants anticipate a 10 percent increase in sales volume with the influx of school students and teachers, which has increased property values and rents.[4] Now, the school system, City Hall, and local businesses are exploring opportunities for coordinated planning, including housing for families and teachers.[5] In Trenton, the school system is expanding the process of designing the four school sites to include six more.

COL results in New Jersey demonstrate that school systems are willing to rethink school design for the 21st century. Citizens do not want learning facilities locked up in isolated, freestanding buildings; they want students and teachers involved in community life. School programming and design can be integrated with community planning and development.

COL affirms the role of teachers and students as active agents in the creation of our communities. With neighborhood spaces designed for them, their social, intellectual, and economic capital is made available for community development and capacity building. This casts students and teachers as agents of positive community change, an outcome that should help reverse public alienation from and dissatisfaction with public schools.

As the nation spends billions on new and renovated schools, the potential of this investment becomes clear. Unleashed from the box of the school building, these billions can revive towns and cities by leveraging an untapped resource: the power of teachers and learners. This power is visible in Union City, where students and teachers mix with residents of the affordable housing project to help create a safe, sociable community, and in Paterson, where they contribute to the bustle of downtown. It will become visible in Trenton, when a new series of schools share services and amenities with the public. And, if fully realized, it will help reverse decades of decline in both our cities and our public schools.

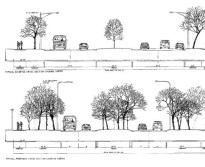

Education and the Urban Landscape: Illinois Institute of Technology

Peter Lindsay Schaudt
Peter Lindsay Schaudt Landscape Architecture, Inc.

Introduction

With the changing complexity of urban life and educational institutions, it seems imperative that rather than setting institutions apart we should be bringing them together. We should find ways to link city with school and join key institutions through the infrastructure of the city. The Illinois Institute of Technology (IIT) "urban landscape" project plays an important role in *connecting* people to each other and *connecting* complex programmatic uses *on* a campus *in* a city.[1]

Illinois Institute of Technology, Chicago, Illinois

Aerial view of the State Street corridor looking north

Sections through State Street

Before and after sketches of the new boulevard

View of the completed, nascent boulevard

What do education and the urban landscape have in common? Higher education has changed since Thomas Jefferson's classic architectural model of the University of Virginia: an idealized arrangement of buildings with the library in command of both academic life and nature. This scheme exemplified a relationship between knowledge and the natural world. The concept of this American campus icon is used to this day on small rural college campuses as an ideal for urban design in new settings. What about the urban school in a city where nature is designed and constructed? Mies van der Rohe's IIT campus was a transformation of Jefferson's paradigm. As architect and curator Phyllis Lambert has noted:

"While Mies established a major central greensward space, it flowed like water around stones into the open and compressed spaces created by buildings sliding past one another."[2] This design was equally novel for the way in which the campus was brought into relationship with the urban fabric.

Background

A successful urban landscape is a biological and social conduit of urban life, constantly flowing like an artery or a river. A cohesive urban landscape is structured by public infrastructure, creating good accessibility and adjacent architectural programs activating the outside space, lending purpose and functionality to the routines of daily life. Chicago has a tradition of boulevards that, when first designed, served this civic purpose in the large urban structure. Not only are they a part of Chicago's historical legacy, the landscaped boulevards have stimulated neighborhood development and revitalization. In European cultures, Haussmann's transformation of 19th-century Paris inspired a new concept of boulevards for structuring the urban setting. His work improved natural light and ventilation, bringing a piece of strongly landscaped infrastructure into an existing city. In America, architects and planners of the City Beautiful movement incorporated parks and boulevards to spark real estate development and to structure both transportation and recreation in new and existing cities. Frederick Law Olmsted first designed the boulevard system in Chicago in the 1870s. This network of recreational parks was later augmented and extended by important Chicago landscape architects such as Jens Jensen. The boulevards eventually became incorporated in Daniel Burnham's and Edward H. Bennett's monumental 1909 *Plan of Chicago*. As urban historian Daniel Bluestone notes: "Spinning their way through the city, the boulevards joined the parks and the city as the warp and woof of real estate development and creative urbanism."[3]

Design Reinterpreted and Translated

Two years ago, a five-block transformation of State Street took place between 30th and 35th Streets. This section intersects Mies van der Rohe's historic Illinois Institute of Technology (IIT) campus.[4] What is often referred to as "Mies's" campus had been part of the federal government's plan for urban renewal in the Bronzeville neighborhood in the 1940s, as IIT was expanded from the original Armour Institute into a campus of buildings and infrastructure in an open, parklike setting. The buildings of the IIT campus are now nearly 50 years old. Additionally, deferred landscape maintenance over the last 30 years has created a bland, tired-looking landscape that does not reflect the original design intent.

Today, revitalization is seen as a layering of interdisciplinary exchanges, programmatic integration, and a view of the landscape as something more than the decoration of pragmatic municipal services. This relationship between the built and the natural gave meaning to the IIT campus, an urban space defined as much by Mies's buildings as by the landscape spaces that open among them. The landscape of the IIT campus represents the legacy of Alfred Caldwell (1903–1998). Caldwell was a landscape architect, teacher, and protégé of Jens Jensen who collaborated with Mies for years at IIT. Caldwell was IIT's landscape architect when Mies's buildings were erected in the 1940s. Although Caldwell never fully developed a landscape master plan for the campus, his design concepts have strongly influenced the collective thinking in the IIT community: "According to [Mies's colleague Peter] Carter, Caldwell had found a parallel between 'Jensen's insistence on the integrity of nature and Mies van der Rohe's insistence on the honest expression of a building's structure', so that the 'interaction between this free-flowing landscaping, with its diaphanous honey locusts and substantial hawthorn, and the pristine architecture, contributes a kind of poetry to both exterior and interior milieu'."[5] Caldwell designed and planted many landscape "pieces" around campus. Yet, only two planting plans were among Caldwell's materials in the IIT archive. Not surprisingly, they were for Mies's most famous IIT buildings, Crown Hall and the chapel.

Although Mies's design called for a continuous flow between the landscaped open space, elevated rail tracks just east of State Street divided the east and west sides of the IIT campus into two 60-acre halves, academic on one side and residential on the other. The fragmented condition of the campus led to a recent international competition for a new student center that would "bind" the two halves. Rem Koolhaas's winning scheme creates an east-west connection for the campus. The building literally extends below the El tracks and features a "tube" that envelops the tracks from above, mitigating the deafening noise of the trains.

State Street is one of the major north-south streets connecting the Loop to the South Side of Chicago. One of the main projects that initiated IIT's recommitment of public space was the need to upgrade this significant major urban artery. This urban landscape component of the revitalization is a simple, yet radical, solution: eliminate the on-street parking on both sides of a median boulevard and enlarge the parkway width, subsequently allowing for a reinterpretation of the historical landscape by Caldwell. The lack of archival information for this space required the design team to reinterpret and translate his designs for other parts of the campus. The planting plan by Caldwell for Crown Hall in 1956 offered a solution, slightly undulating tree spacing. The fact that the trees alongside Crown Hall are nearly 50 years old makes this effect visually understandable. In the redesign of State Street, the trees are spaced approximately 16 to 18 feet apart and are offset between 1 and 2 feet in the lateral direction for a distance of five blocks. This creates a north-south landscaped boulevard and, as the trees mature, an east-west fusion is created through the foliage arching over the street.

This design avoids the ubiquitous gateway solution to a school, as the campus is open at all sides. The landscape is the urban introduction to the educational community, a visual experience of being immersed into a tree canopy corridor. Transparency at eye level is enhanced with only large shade trees pruned and no midsize flower trees obscuring views through the landscape.[6]

The cross section describes the project in two simple drawings. The new design keeps the sidewalk at 8 feet and expands the parkway from 11 to 22 feet wide, thus eliminating the on-street parking. Both north and southbound lanes are maintained at 22-foot widths, and the median width remains 23 feet.

Conclusion

This project is novel and important within the context of Chicago because it recognizes two historical periods and landscape idioms: Olmsted, Jensen, and Burnham's late-19th-century boulevard system on the one hand, and Caldwell and Mies's mid-20th-century landscape of openness and extension on the other. Furthermore, the historical significance of Miesian architecture and design principles within Chicago compelled the designers to understand and find a way to preserve and reintegrate modern landscape design into a larger urban framework. Although this project is for a college campus, it establishes principles in which landscape and open space may be used to integrate educational spaces into the larger functional and symbolic structure of a neighborhood or a city. Further, it suggests ways in which private educational institutions can use their resources and history to enhance significant pieces of public space.

The relationship between the classroom and the patios is not achieved using windows. The large prefabricated concrete pieces and laminated glass enclosure allow for a great deal of transparency while at the same time creating a fair amount of privacy due to the dimensions of the crosspieces. By not having windows, there is no element of scale from which the children could compare themselves.

—Xavier Vendrell

Riumar Elementary School,
Tarragona, Spain,
Ruisanchez-Vendrell
Architects, 1997,
exterior view and student
installation

II

Case Studies

Prototypes and Paratypes: Future Studies

Sharon Haar
School of Architecture, University of Illinois at Chicago

Flying into almost any airport in North America, one has an opportunity to overview the physical characteristics of educational institutions: from the landlocked urban school with its small play lot, often built in relation-ship to a small community park, to the sprawling suburban school with its vast quantity of playing fields and parking lots. These buildings come in a variety of forms—known to architects as "typologies"—ranging from the multistory urban school in a tight "E" or "H" configuration to the single-story suburban school with dispersed classrooms and a multitude of community facilities. Beyond the specific features of an individual school, however, is its relationship to the surrounding community—its urban morphology. Does the school stand apart through a distant, imposing monumentality, or does it blend into its neighborhood, integrating land-scapes and spaces for community life? These buildings are recognizable because so many of them, at first glance, seem alike. Modules of classrooms, consistent use of similar durable materials, relationships of classrooms repeating down long hallways, playground equipment, ball fields...not to mention the repetitive urban grid or the endless networks of suburban streets...the careful eye identifies patterns associated with the student's own educational experiences. The reverse is true as well. The word "school" conjures specific images and memories for each of us.

Crow Island Elementary
School, Winnetka, Illinois,
Perkins, Wheeler and Will
with Eliel & Eero Saarinen,
1940

Friedrich L. Jahn School,
Chicago, Illinois,
Dwight H. Perkins, Chicago
Public Schools, 1908

79

Are all schools alike? Is there a "prototypical" ideal or are some of the best schools in some form "paratypes," responses to specific student and community identities and conditions? Certainly, there are known typological groupings of schools. For instance, urban schools of the early 20th century were developed into shape-specific typologies that could address common morphological conditions. In dense fabric conditions, school forms often varied according to their location within a block. Each condition—an entire block, the corner, the center—led to a different, although often repeated solution, in order to solve problems of light and air, interior and exterior circulation, the approach to places of assembly (auditoriums and gymnasiums), and the expression of monumentality that would signal an institution of urban life. Where they still exist, these schools are seen as either historical landmarks or as decaying, outdated facilities. Sometimes they are both. By contrast, suburban schools of the 1950s and 1960s were more often organized and shaped by function than by the specifics of a context. Characterized by access to greater quantities of land, and in the beginning, more choice in where the school might be placed, these schools were more likely to dematerialize into their land-scapes, as individual functions acquired individual forms: classroom wings, a gym opening out into vast playing fields, a courtyard space for office functions. Where schools were the first institutions of public life, they often acquired facilities that could replicate the institutions of the city: libraries, community centers, performance spaces, and swimming pools, becoming vast, independent campuses. These schools are seen as community centers, or as precursors to suburban sprawl. It depends on your perspective.

As education itself is a large, complex discipline, architecture for education has become a large, complex specialty of the architecture pro-fession. The design of educational institutions merits its own AIA committee and is dominated by large firms with long legacies in school buildings that assess "best practices." With few exceptions, the tendency to treat schools as their own category of public investment makes integra-tive urban approaches rare. Every generation has its own compendium of case studies and primers, largely designed to guide communities in the design and planning of their new schools. In these "how to" guides the building is often treated as an object in relationship to the pool of students; exemplary projects rarely show the school building in its context. Design occurs from the statistics out; architecture is treated as an aesthetic, and "flexibility" in relationship to varying curricular circumstances or community needs is treated as an abstraction. Schools of today, however, need to be more than flexible; they need to be truly interdisciplinary, not only in the curricula that they provide, but also in the ways in which they incorporate the larger needs of the community, expanding the definition of who is a student.

Many people ascribe the use of "prototypes" to school architecture developed in the heyday of high modernism. In fact, to the extent that the modern school is a derivative of the development of mass education, American school architecture has always been based on some concept of prototypical design. The prototype is a leftover of modernism; the belief that with enough study and refinement of a program one can find an enduring exemplar for future needs. Despite continual changes in curricular and student needs, prototypical components—if not identical school buildings—will remain with us. Many advances can be made through prototyping, but architects must challenge themselves to engage these sophisticated "kits of parts" into the community, create individual identities for each school, and respond to the specific needs of a given neighborhood and its students.

By contrast, we need to remember that, in some respects, educators who believe that education can take place anywhere are correct. Despite its many repetitive elements, the school container is malleable. The finest classroom on a pleasant spring day may be under a large tree canopy. But in the middle of winter in the Midwest, broken windows and an aged heating system will make learning difficult. We know that classrooms can be located in skyscrapers, abandoned malls and warehouses, and former townhouses. But this is not because the building doesn't matter. In each of these instances the context is an equal player in the educational event. Similarly, students, teachers, and parents alike must take active roles in incorporating the environment into educational experience. Education becomes activity.

What architectural elements play the leading role in the development of a school: the classroom module, structural bay, prefabricated wall system? And how are these affected by changes that transform the students' relationships to teachers, peers, or community? How are new communications infrastructures changing today's classrooms and students' relationships to them? Are schools, perhaps, ideal places to demonstrate the future of green buildings and a greater ecological approach to the environment?

These are all valid questions, and it is difficult to assign priority to one over another in all instances. The building will, inevitably, have to sit in its context and adjust to its site, its users, and specific community needs. We must not forget, however, that these are primarily spaces for children. Equally as important, even as our urban environments are becoming increasingly similar (and isn't that alone a reason why schools should be different?), architectural technology is moving from prototyping to paratyping. Information technology is changing how buildings are designed and how they are built; efficiencies can be obtained through information transfer of individual instances. Schools of the future will combine both prototypical and paratypical approaches and elements, the best of what we know about design for education, and suggestions for the future, integrating new digital and ecological technologies, new social constructions, and new ways of constructing knowledge.

In the examples illustrated here the specificity of each condition defies the possibility of building prototype solutions, but offers lessons on models of partnership, where the development of the urban fabric is more than just an aesthetic gesture. As a result, the following studies are presented as paratypes: not as models for imitation, but as examples that stand aside from the type. They are projects that are "in the works" suggesting ways in which school design is transforming to affect urban and neighborhood development. In their differences they become exemplars, each for the way in which the architecture is used as the interface between the space of the school and the space of the larger community. They represent change at multiple scales of infrastructure:

physical/visual/urban and digital/invisible/internal.

Finally, we must remember that schools do not lose their significance as institutions because the significance of institutions is disappearing in our postindustrial, networked environment. In fact, if museums or libraries can be used as examples, the cultural and social role of institutions has only expanded in this more diverse and diffuse environment. These case studies demonstrate that it is the role of architecture and educators to steer clear of the impulse to design the ideal container for the ideal curriculum. The history of the design of educational communities illustrates that schools offer an opportunity to think idealistically while accomplishing pragmatic goals. This suggests that we should not reduce the design of schools to the economic and engineering protocols of our underground infrastructures but rather create an architecture to celebrate the possibility of the new knowledge and interaction at the root of contemporary, progressive educational initiatives.

Aerial view of finished design showing New Technology & Design Center, student center, and theater expansion

View from I-280 showing the windmills on the interstate façade

84

Lick-Wilmerding High School, San Francisco

Pfau Architecture Ltd. San Francisco, California

Lick-Wilmerding High School is a nonprofit, independent, coeducational, college preparatory day school at the southern edge of San Francisco along I-280. It integrates an academic curriculum with a distinctive program in the technical and fine arts. Pfau Architecture's expansion of the school's facilities, the winning entry in an invited design competition, includes a new technology and design center and enlarged and renovated space for the performing arts, the student center, and a new cafeteria, while incorporating sustainable building technologies.

View from field level looking out from the hill

The architects describe the project: "The new landscape design and building forms are inseparable. Exterior spaces, which were once ambiguous, become programmatically charged. Roofs of shops are transformed into terraced landscapes: A raised portion of undulating roofscape in front of the cafeteria, The Hill, becomes a place to enjoy the view while catching an outdoor lunch. A sculpture garden between the theater and the original classroom building acts as a place where new planting areas and a walking path provide a backdrop for a rotation of student outdoor exhibits."

New and old technologies are combined in the new organization of the campus. The new programmatic elements preserve portions of the existing school campus and its relationship to the surrounding community while signaling the commitment to ecological technologies through photovoltaic panels, louvered sun control elements, and a proposed bank of windmills located to be seen from the interstate.

Site plan

Washington Heights School, "U" proposal

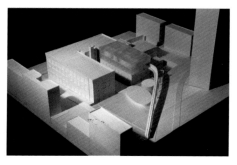

Architecture of Adjustment, New York City

kOnyk architecture Brooklyn, New York

kOnyk architecture's NYC Public School Overcrowding Design Study looked at three existing, overutilized schools in New York City with the intention of devising "immediate solutions for temporarily overcrowded conditions." The proposals expand existing prototype buildings in "U," "O," and "X" configurations.

The proposal for PS 152 added a new kindergarten with a separate entrance to the upper story of an early-20th-century building on a congested site in Washington Heights. A new addition at the rear of the building contains a gymnasium, auditorium, and library spaces. Its roof becomes a new landscape for a play yard. The movement of these elements out of the original building frees up space for new classroom and teacher spaces.

The proposal for PS 33, the Chelsea School, in Manhattan involves adding a significant new structure to an existing midcentury building that is a diagonal object on its square block. The strategy involves the design of a "ring" of new classrooms, teacher offices, and reading rooms to surround the older building. The new configuration results in three interior courtyard spaces and a "perforated" rooftop playground.

This project was funded by the New York State Council on the Arts and sponsored by the Architectural League of New York.

Chelsea School, "X" proposal

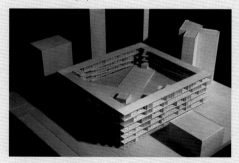

Project model, "loft" spaces that house the making and presentation of art "rotate" around the amphitheater

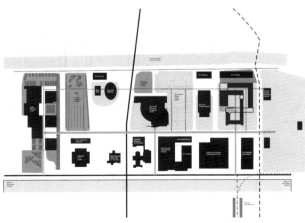

Site diagram of the arts district

Booker T. Washington School for the Performing and Visual Arts, Dallas

Allied Works Architecture Inc. Portland, Oregon

Allied Works' winning design for the expansion of the Booker T. Washington School in Dallas utilizes the landscape and spaces for performance, creation, and exhibition of student work to form an integral connection with its surroundings and the public. The school is intended to anchor existing and planned institutions in a growing arts district. An outdoor amphitheater, accessible from a forecourt shared with surrounding institutions, serves as a central space for the school. The project preserves the public presence and identity of the historic school building while incorporating it into the formal and programmatic organization of the enlarged facility. As the architects of the project state: "The new building is held in tension between the spatial forces focusing in (centripetal) and extending out (centrifugal), between the work of the students and the presentation to the public."

Booker T. Washington was the first African American high school in Dallas and has served as a magnet school for the arts since 1976. Its program includes academic, visual arts, music, theater, and dance components. The competition for the expansion of the school was funded in part by the New Public Works program of the National Endowment for the Arts. The school will be a vital component of active life in the arts district, an infrastructure of existing and new buildings by internationally renowned architects including Renzo Piano, Rem Koolhaas, and Norman Foster.

Public entry

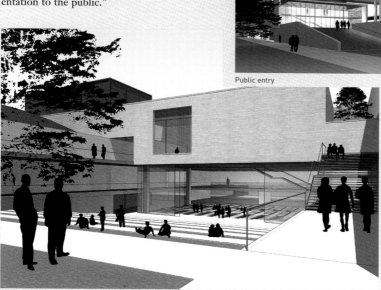

Courtyard

Elementary school using abandoned mall structure

Play lot

Abandoned mall

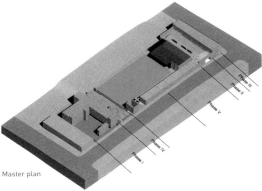

Master plan

90

Camino Nuevo Middle School, Los Angeles

Daley, Genik Architects Santa Monica, California

The Camino Nuevo Charter Academy, founded by Pueblo Nuevo, a community support group in Westlake, provides education for elementary and middle school students. The master plan for the campus anticipates four phases that, when completed, will occupy almost an entire block near MacArthur Park in Los Angeles. To date, the elementary school, a portion of the middle school, and a play lot are complete. A performing arts school will follow.

The project is notable for the way in which the clients and their architects utilize existing pieces of the urban fabric to mobilize local redevelopment. The elementary school is located in a renovated L-shaped mini-mall, whose shape and size suits the classroom and circulation needs of the school. The former parking lot is now the school courtyard used for outdoor assembly and play. A portion of the middle school, as well as auxiliary spaces, is located in a former bow-string-truss warehouse; a second phase will take over an adjacent abandoned office building. An "interior street" in the warehouse allows light to enter the deep building, while exposing components of the original structure. A play lot is created in a former empty lot next to the elementary school.

The new school creates new uses for abandoned spaces in a dense and impoverished portion of the city. The introduction of synthetic recyled lumber lattices, colorful stucco, and new green and hard-surface play spaces reinvigorate the site and create inviting spaces for the community.

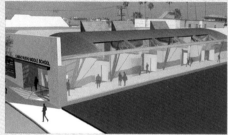
Middle school building

Interior "street" in the middle school building

Oscar DePriest Elementary School, adjacent to Columbus Park on the Far West Side, Chicago.

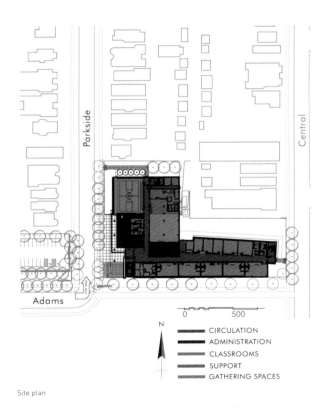

Parkside

Central

Adams

```
0        500
```

N

CIRCULATION
ADMINISTRATION
CLASSROOMS
SUPPORT
GATHERING SPACES

Site plan

Elementary School Prototypes, Chicago Public Schools

OWP/P Architects Chicago, Illinois

To alleviate overcrowded schools expeditiously, Chicago Public Schools asked OWP/P Architects to create a new elementary school prototype that provides learning environments of consistent quality, size, and technology. The benefits of this prototypical program are the ability to maintain control over construction quality, cost, safety, and maintenance within a high quality of building and community design. The "kit of parts" adapts to various site conditions, limits the amount of land acquisition, and reduces the displacement of students in existing facilities during new construction. The design is able to adapt to different sites, population needs, and neighborhoods.

Library interior

Both Anderson Academy and Edward "Duke" Ellington Elementary School have been sited so that the new schools are built around the existing facilities. This keeps the students from being displaced during construction. Oscar DePriest Elementary School is sited so that the academic classrooms open up to adjacent Columbus Park. Each incarnation of the design furnishes gathering spaces of various sizes and configurations, which provide flexibility, opportunity for community use, and an ability to extend the learning environment beyond the classroom. A green roof and solar panels have been designed for implementation at each school. This will facilitate the exploration of sustainability as part of the school curriculum. The design allows for independent access to the libraries, whose form is celebrated in all the buildings.

Anderson Community Academy

Edward "Duke" Ellington Elementary School

Bibliography

Image Credits

Contributors

**MICD Session
Participants**

Endnotes

Bibliography

Alan, Richard. "Work in Progress: An Architect's Vision for Transforming Abandoned or Neglected Downtown Buildings into Thriving Public Schools Is Reshaping the City of Paterson, N.J." *Education Week* (June 21, 2000), 1, 40–46.

The Architectural League of New York. *New Schools New York: Plans and Precedents for Small Schools*. New York: Princeton Architectural Press, 1992.

Beaumont, Constance E. *Smart States, Better Communities: How State Governments Can Help Citizens Preserve Their Communities*. Washington, D.C.: National Trust for Historic Preservation, 1996.

Betsky, Aaron and Julie Eizenberg. *KoningEizenberg: Buildings*. New York: Rizzoli International Publishers, 1996.

Boyer, Ernest. *Ready to Learn: A Mandate for the Nation*. Princeton: The Carnegie Foundation for the Advancement of Learning, 1991, 91–97.

Branch, Mark Alden. "Tomorrow's Schoolhouse: Making the Pieces Work." *Progressive Architecture* 75 (June 1994): 77–83.

Brubaker, C. William. *Planning and Designing Schools: Architecture for Architectural Education by Perkins & Will*. New York: McGraw-Hill Inc., 1998.

Ceppi, Giulio and Michele Zini. *Children, Spaces, Relations: Metaproject for an Environment for Young Children*. Italy: Reggio Children s. r. l., 1998.

Corner, James. *School Power*. New York: The Free Press, 1995.

Dewey, John. *Democracy and Education*. New York: The Free Press, 1965.

Dudek, Mark. *Architecture of Schools: The New Learning Environments*. Boston: Architectural Press, 2000.

Fisher, Thomas. "No Cure-Alls for K–12." *Architectural Record* 185 (October 1997): 105–112.

"Focus on: Refresher Courses For Schools." *Architectural Record* 181 (August 1993): 116–119.

Graves, Ben E. *School Ways: The Planning and Design of America's Schools*. New York: McGraw-Hill, Inc., 1993.

Grunenberg, Christoph and Sheila Kennedy. *Material Misuse*. London: Architectural Association, 2001.

Kozol, Jonathan. *Alternative Schools: A Guide for Educators and Parents*. New York: Continuum, 1982 [1972].

Lightfoot, Sarah Lawrence. *The Good High School: Portraits of Character and Culture*. New York: Basic Books, 1983.

Meier, Deborah. *The Power of Their Ideas: Lessons for America from a Small School in Harlem*. Boston: Beacon Press, 1995.

Murphy, Jim. "P/A Inquiry: Schools." *Progressive Architecture* 72 (July 1991): 86–93.

Pearson, Clifford. "Essay: K–12 Schools." *Architectural Record* 189 (February 2001): 131–148.

——. "Overhauling Education." *Architectural Record* 181 (August 1993): 82–83.

Programme on Educational Building. *Schools for Today and Tomorrow: An International Compendium of Exemplary Educational Facilities*. Washington, D.C.: OECD Publications and Information Centre, 1996.

Sanoff, Henry. *School Design*. New York: Van Nostrand Reinhold, 1994.

Scogin, Mack and Merrill Elam. *The Work of Scogin, Elam & Bray, Architects*. Ann Arbor, Michigan: University of Michigan College of Architecture and Urban Planning, 1999.

Sizer, Theodore. *Horace's School: Redesigning the American High School*. Boston: Houghton Mifflin, 1992.

Strickland, Roy. "Architectural Alternatives to the Post-World War II Public School: Designs by the New American School Design Project." *Architectural Research Centers Applied Research in Architecture and Planning* 2 (Spring 1996): 61–79.

——. ed. *Designing a City of Learning: Paterson, NJ*. Cambridge, Massachusetts: New American School Design Project, 2001.

——. "Designing the New American School: Schools for an Urban Neighborhood." *Columbia University Teachers College Record* 96 (Fall 1994): 34–57.

——. "Neighborhoods for Learning." *Places* 11 (Winter 2000): 58–65.

"Two Urban Schools," *Architectural Review* 189 (September 1991): 39–47.

Urban Planning Bureau of the City of Vienna. *The New Schoolhouse: Schoolchild's Universe and Urban Particle*. Berlin: Verlag A.F. Koska, 1996.

Image Credits

Web Sites

Architectural Record Building Types Study on Schools: *www.architecturalrecord.com*, Building Types Study 794

Chicago Public Schools Design Competition: *www.schooldesigncomp.org/ indexold.htm*

Coalition for Community Schools: *www.communityschools.org/new.html*; *www.communitiyschools.org/ pubs.partners.html*

National Trust for Historic Preservation: *www.nationaltrust.org/issues*

Universal Design: *www.design.ncsu.edu; www.cae.org.uk*

U.S. Department of Education: *www.ed.gov/about/pubs.jsp*; *www.ed.gov/inits/construction/ ctty-centers.html*

Cover: Courtesy of Walter Leedy.

3: Photo by Roberta Dupuis-Devlin, Photographic Services, UIC.

10 (top): From Walter Dwight Moody, *What of the City?* Chicago: A. C. McClurg & Co., 1919.

10 (bottom): From The High School Students of New York City, *Our City—New York: A Book on City Government*. New York: Allyn and Bacon, 1924.

13: Courtesy of David Dodt and Greg Lauterback.

14 (top two rows): Photos by Roberta Dupuis-Devlin, Photographic Services, UIC.

14 (bottom row)–23: Courtesy of Schools as Catalysts for Community Development Participants.

26: Courtesy of South Carolina Coastal Conservation League.

28: Courtesy of Bassetti Architects, photo by David Melody.

30: Courtesy of Constance E. Beaumont.

31 top: Courtesy of Walter Leedy.

31 inset: Courtesy of Lee Batdorff, Common Ground Communities.

34–38, 40: Courtesy of Business and Professional People for the Public Interest, photos by Jon Randolph.

39 top: Courtesy of Marble · Fairbanks Architects.

39 bottom: Courtesy of KoningEizenberg Architecture.

42–51: Courtesy of Kennedy & Violich Architecture; p. 47: photo by William Traub; p. 48: photo by Bruce T. Martin.

52–59: Courtesy of KoningEizenberg Architecture, photos by Benny Chan.

60–69: Courtesy of Roy Strickland; p. 60: drawing by Kiran Mathema; p. 65 (bottom): drawing by John Dimitriov; p. 66 (top): drawing by Li Lian Tan; p. 66 (bottom): drawing by Timothy Jones.

70: Courtesy of Peter Lindsay Schaudt Landscape Architecture; upper left photo by Peter Schaudt; lower left sketches by Bruce Bondy; lower right photo by Chandra Goldsmith.

78: Photos by Sharon Haar.

84–85: Courtesy of Pfau Architecture Ltd.

86–87: Courtesy of kOnyk architecture.

88–89: Courtesy of Allied Works Architecture.

90–91: Courtesy of Daly, Genik Architects, photos by Tom Bonner.

92–93: Courtesy of OWP/P Architects and Chicago Public Schools.

Contributors

Constance E. Beaumont is Director for State and Local Policy at the National Trust for Historic Preservation. In this capacity, she has written extensively about state and local public policies affecting historic preservation, land use, urban planning, growth management, and transportation. She has a special interest in the development of alternatives to urban sprawl and is the author of *How Superstore Sprawl Can Harm Communities (And What Citizens Can Do About It)* (1994), *Smart States, Better Communities* (1996), *Better Models for Superstores: Alternatives to Big-Box Sprawl* (1997), and *Challenging Sprawl, Organizational Responses to a National Problem* (1999).

Julie Eizenberg is founding Principal with Hank Koning of KoningEizenberg Architecture in Santa Monica, California. In practice for over 20 years, KoningEizenberg has become well known for small buildings for everyday living including affordable housing, community and recreation centers, schools, custom homes, hotels, stores, and workplaces. KoningEizenberg Architecture has received recognition for its work in housing and community-based projects, receiving awards such as the *Progressive Architecture* First Award and National AIA Honor Awards for affordable housing. In 1999, the firm received the City of Santa Monica's Sustainable Design Award, the Los Angeles AIA (Merit Award) and the California AIA (Honor Award) for PS#1 Elementary School, a progressive, small elementary school in Santa Monica. Eizenberg has also taught at UCLA's Graduate School of Architecture & Urban Planning, as well as at Yale School of Architecture, MIT, and the Graduate School of Design at Harvard.

Sharon Haar, Director of the Mayors' Institute on City Design: Schools as Catalysts for Community Development, is an architect and Assistant Professor at the University of Illinois at Chicago School of Architecture where she teaches studios and courses focused on housing and urban design. Her projects and articles have been published in various journals including *Architectural Design, Sites, Newsline*, and the *Harvard Design Magazine*. She is author of "Coming Home: A Postscript on Postmodernism," in *Not At Home*, "Location, Location, Location: Gender and the Archaeology of Urban Settlement," in the *Journal of Architectural Education*, and "At Home in Public: The Hull House Settlement and the Study of the City," in *Embodied Utopias*. She is currently working on a book titled *The City as Campus: Sites of Urban Education* that explores the relationship between urban design and urban universities. She has also taught at Parsons School of Design in New York.

Sheila Kennedy is a Principal of Kennedy & Violich Architecture, a professional practice that explores new possibilities for public architecture and urbanism. The work of Kennedy & Violich Architecture has involved industrial manufacturers, educators, community leaders, and public agencies in projects that explore how elements of infrastructure can be integrated with architecture to express the visible and invisible connections that link people, activities, and spaces in contemporary American culture. Their projects include the Interim Bridges Prototype, the Canton Elementary School, the Madden Dance Theatre and Gym, and a public plaza at the Jackson School at Union Square. Her research and built work have received two AIA awards, as well as awards from *Progressive Architecture*, The Architectural League of New York, The LEF Foundation, and the National Endowment for the Arts. Kennedy is Associate Professor of Architecture at the Harvard Graduate School of Design, where she has taught since 1992.

Cindy S. Moelis and Beth Valukas: Cindy S. Moelis is the Director of Education Initiatives at Business and Professional People for the Public Interest (BPI), one of the sponsoring organizations of the Chicago Public Schools Design Competition. Beth Valukas is a BPI Polikoff-Gautreaux Fellow. Cindy and Beth are lawyers who advocate for quality public education in Chicago. BPI is a public interest law and policy center dedicated to equal justice and to enhancing the quality and equity of life for all people living in the Chicago region. The organization has been actively involved in working to improve the public school system in Chicago for over a decade. In recent years, this work has focused on advocating for the development of small and intimate learning environments, based on a strong and growing body of research demonstrating the positive impacts of such environments on student achievement, teacher satisfaction, and parent involvement.

Leah Ray, Program Coordinator for the Mayors' Institute on City Design: Schools as Catalysts for Community Development, is an Adjunct Associate Professor at the University of Illinois at Chicago School of Architecture where she teaches within the theory curriculum. She received a master of design studies in the history and theory of architecture degree from the Harvard Graduate School of Design, and her current research focuses on the reciprocal relationship between cinema and contemporary architectural design. Her writings include "The Carnivalization of Architecture," "Cities, History, and Memory," and a forthcoming piece entitled "Opposing Mies: the Triangular Constructs of Harry Weese" in *Chicago Is History*, a compilation of essays focusing on Chicago's untold architectural histories to be published by the University of Chicago Press.

Mark Robbins is the Director of Design at the National Endowment for the Arts, where he has undertaken an aggressive program to strengthen the presence of design in the public realm. In addition to efforts to expand grant opportunities he has instituted new Leadership Initiatives including New Public Works, which supports national design competitions. Collectively, these activities have doubled the available funding for design programs. Robbins is an architect and an artist and maintains a practice that encompasses installations, curatorial projects, and teaching. He was formerly an Associate Professor in the Knowlton School of Architecture at The Ohio State University and Curator of Architecture at Ohio State's Wexner Center for the Arts.

Peter Lindsay Schaudt founded the firm of Peter Lindsay Schaudt Landscape Architecture, Inc., in 1991. The firm is dedicated to landscape design excellence and quality service at all scales. Known for collaborations with architects, the firm's work is marked by restraint and elegance, delivering beauty in design elements that are sculpted and abstracted into a quiet simplicity. Ongoing projects include the Landscape Master Plan for the historic Mies van der Rohe Illinois Institute of Technology campus, the new Tennessee Titans stadium in Nashville, Tennessee, and Prairie Crossing, a 667-acre "conservation community" in Grayslake, Illinois. Other projects include campus and community master plans, public parks, and several private residences. The firm's resume also includes two award-winning projects: a garden at Chicago's Midway Plaisance in Washington Park and the Grayslake Central Park Site Plan in Grayslake, Illinois.

Roy Strickland is Director of the New American School Design Project at the Taubman College of Architecture and Urban Planning at the University of Michigan. His work is concerned with the development of design studies, workshops, conferences, and publications that correlate discussion of K–12 educational reform with architectural design. His school-design workshop was contracted by the Berkeley (California) Unified School District to provide master plan concepts and design guidelines for the $160 million redevelopment of the 7500 student public system and by the Six Schools Complex in Washington, D.C., to develop architectural concepts for the expansion and rehabilitation of its facilities. Currently, the workshop is making design and planning recommendations for Paterson, New Jersey's $500–800 million school-building initiative. In his practice, he has also designed and programmed residential, museum, public space, and urban design projects that have been published in the *New York Times*, *Architectural Record*, and *Progressive Architecture*. He has also taught at the Massachusetts Institute of Technology and Columbia University Graduate School of Architecture, Planning, and Preservation.

MICD Session Participants

Resource Team

Constance E. Beaumont
National Trust for Historic
Preservation

Julie Eizenberg
KoningEizenberg Architecture

Merrill Elam
Mack Scogin Merrill Elam Architects

Sharon Haar, Session Chair
School of Architecture,
University of Illinois at Chicago

Clifford B. Janey
Rochester Public Schools

Sheila Kennedy
Kennedy & Violich Architecture

Judith Russi Kirshner
College of Architecture and the Arts,
University of Illinois at Chicago

Katerina Rüedi Ray
School of Architecture,
University of Illinois at Chicago

Leah Ray
School of Architecture,
University of Illinois at Chicago

Mark Robbins
National Endowment for the Arts

Jane M. Saks
College of Architecture and the Arts,
University of Illinois at Chicago

Peter Lindsay Schaudt
Peter Lindsay Schaudt Landscape
Architecture, Inc.

Roy Strickland
Taubman College of Architecture
and Urban Planning, University
of Michigan

Participating Mayors

Kirk Humphreys
Oklahoma City, Oklahoma

Bob Knight
Wichita, Kansas

Dannel P. Malloy
Stamford, Connecticut

Patrick J. McManus
Lynn, Massachusetts

Daniel C. Snarr
Murray City, Utah

Judith Valles
San Bernardino, California

Chicago Panelists

Avram Lothan, Moderator
DeStefano & Partners

William Ayers
College of Education,
University of Illinois at Chicago

Carol Ross Barney
Ross Barney + Jankowski

Roberta Feldman
City Design Center,
University of Illinois at Chicago

Timothy Martin
Chicago Public Schools

Adrian Smith, FAIA
Skidmore, Owings & Merrill

Jane Tompkins
College of Education,
University of Illinois at Chicago

Endnotes

Schools for Cities: Urban Strategies,
Sharon Haar

1   Stephanie Banchero, "School
    Buildings a Growth Industry,"
    Chicago Tribune (September 21,
    1999). See also Mark Alden
    Branch, "Tomorrow's Schoolhouse:
    Making the Pieces Fit," *Progressive
    Architecture* 75 (June 1994): 77–83.
    Branch notes that there are politi-
    cal motivations, such as the ability
    to find financial backing, for
    enlarging the number of individuals
    who will have access to a school.
2   Jeanne Silver Frankl, "Advocacy
    and Architecture," *New Schools for
    New York* (New York: Princeton
    Architectural Press, 1992), 17. New
    Schools for New York was a design
    ideas competition sponsored by the
    Architectural League of New York
    in the late 1980s. Several of the
    projects that resulted from this
    program formed the basis of real
    projects in the 1990s.
3   Anthony Vidler, "Different Schools
    of Thought," *Los Angeles Times*
    (February 20, 2000).
4   Dwight H. Perkins was the archi-
    tect of the Chicago Board of
    Education from 1905 to 1910. Like
    his colleague Charles B. Snyder in
    New York, he had a great influence
    on the design of public school
    buildings in the early 20th century.
    Perkins was also closely tied to the
    Arts and Crafts movement, pro-
    gressive cultural and civic causes,
    and John Dewey.
5   John Dewey, the founder of the
    Laboratory School in Chicago,
    advanced the cause of a progressive
    education focusing on experiential
    growth.
6   William Levitt quoted in Frank
    Fogarty, "New Schools for 'Free',"
    Architectural Forum 109 (October
    1958): 121.

7   Herbert J. Gans, *The Levittowners:
    Ways of Life and Politics in a New
    Suburban Community* (New York:
    Pantheon Books, 1967).
8   The physical relationship of
    schools to new housing was a fea-
    ture of suburban developments
    such as Radburn, New Jersey, in
    1920s. The California architect
    Richard J. Neutra began designing
    "community schools" before the
    end of World War II.
9   The "small school movement"
    refers to a pedagogical more than a
    physical concept. Nonetheless, it is
    beginning to have an influence on
    the design of school buildings. For
    a discussion of small schools, see
    Deborah Meier, *The Power of Their
    Ideas: Lessons for America from a
    Small School in Harlem* (Boston:
    Beacon Press, 1995).
10 Business and Professional People
    for the Public Interest was not a
    participant in the original MICD
    sessions, as the Chicago competi-
    tion was just getting underway in
    the winter of 2000.
11 Mildred S. Friedman, "Context for
    Learning," *Design Quarterly* 90/91
    (1974): 9–10.

*Reenvisioning Schools: The Mayors'
Questions,* Leah Ray

1   Unless otherwise noted, quotes are
    taken from the transcripts of the
    MICD: Schools as Catalysts for
    Community Development sympo-
    sium, March 23–25, 2000.

Why Johnny Can't Walk to School,
Constance E. Beaumont

1   To see *Why Johnny Can't Walk to
    School,* the National Trust for
    Historic Preservation's report on
    public policies affecting school
    facilities, visit *http://www.national-
    trust.org/issues/historic_schools.html.*

2   "Case 13: Lincoln, Nebraska,
    Public School Systems: The
    Advance Scouts for Urban Sprawl,"
    in Richard K. Olson and Thomas
    A. Lyon, *Under the Blade: The
    Conversion of Agricultural Landscapes*
    (Boulder, Colorado: Westview
    Press, 1999), 370.
3   Telephone interview with Dan
    Becker, September 2000.
4   Statement by Lakis Polycarpou
    at November 16, 2000 press
    conference held by the National
    Trust for Historic Preservation
    at Murch Elementary School in
    Washington, D.C.
5   Ibid.

*Lessons from the Chicago Public Schools
Design Competition,* Cindy S. Moelis
with Beth Valukas

1   Karen Fairbanks of Marble ·
    Fairbanks Architects quoted in
    Mike Kennedy, "By Design,"
    American School and University,
    January 1, 2002.
2   A special acknowledgment to
    Jeanne Nowaczewski, Jaime
    Hendrickson and Jennifer
    Salvatore, former BPI staff, as well
    as Pamela Clarke and John Ayers of
    LQE for their exceptional leader-
    ship throughout the Chicago
    competition.
3   See, for example, Patricia A.
    Wasley, Michelle Fine, Matt
    Gladden, Nicole E. Holland,
    Sherry P. King, Esther Mosak, and
    Linda C. Powell, *Small Schools:
    Great Strides, A Study of New Small
    Schools in Chicago* (New York: Bank
    Street College of Education, 2000).
4   The small schools movement was
    well underway in Chicago prior to
    this point. However, 1995 was the
    year that the Chicago School
    Reform Board of Trustees adopted
    a resolution committing to the
    formation and strengthening of
    small schools in Chicago.

5 The South Side site is located in the Roseland community between 103rd and 104th Streets between Wentworth and Princeton Avenues. The North Side site is located in the Irving Park neighborhood at Sacramento and Elston.

6 Competition funders included The Richard H. Driehaus Foundation, the National Endowment for the Arts, Reva and David Logan Foundation, Graham Foundation for Advanced Studies in the Fine Arts, Oppenheimer Family Foundation, Chicago Association of Realtors Educational Foundation, Nuveen Investments, Polk Bros. Foundation, and United Airlines.

7 Pamela Clarke, Leadership for Quality Education; Roberta Feldman, City Design Center, University of Illinois at Chicago; Sunny Fischer, the Richard H. Driehaus Foundation; Ralph Hernandez, Hispanic American Construction Industry Association; Michael Mayo, CPS Board Member; Jeanne Nowaczewski, BPI; Beatriz Rendon, Chicago Public Schools; Donna Robertson, Dean, College of Architecture, Illinois Institute of Technology; and Richard Solomon, Graham Foundation for Advanced Studies in the Fine Arts.

8 The jurors were Dr. William Ayers, University of Illinois at Chicago; Lance Jay Brown, City College of the City University of New York; Marissa Hopkins, Catalyst Marketing Group; Ralph Johnson, Perkins & Will; M. David Lee, Stull & Lee, Inc.; Dr. Giacomo Mancuso, Chicago Public Schools; Linda Owens, Davis Developmental Center; Brigitte Shim, Shim-Sutcliffe Architects; Dr. Richard Smith, Frederick Stock School; Dennis Vail, Langston Hughes School.

9 The four finalists from the open competition were Borum, Daubmann, Hyde & Roddier (formerly known as GROUND Design Studio) (Ann Arbor, Michigan), Marble · Fairbanks Architects (New York, New York), Jack L. Gordon Architects (New York, New York), and Lubrano Ciavarra Design (New York, New York).

10 Specialists brought into the community meetings included Leslie Kanes Weisman, an expert on universal design and sustainability; Dr. William Ayers, a professor of education at the University of Illinois at Chicago; Tom Forman of Chicago Associates Planners and Architects; and architect Michael Iverson.

11 Marble · Fairbanks Architects received the P/A Award sponsored by *Architecture Magazine*, the 2001 American Institute of Architects Project Award in *Oculus*, New York AIA Journal, and was featured in the January 2002 edition of *Architecture*. The winning design submitted by KoningEizenberg Architecture was featured in the January/February 2002 edition of *Metropolitan Home* magazine, the May 2001 edition of *Architectural Record*, and the summer 2001 edition of *Competitions*.

12 *Architecture for Education: New School Designs from the Chicago Competition* will be published by BPI in the fall of 2002. For more information or to obtain a copy, please contact BPI at (312) 641-5570 or *http://www.bpichicago.org*.

The City of Learning: Schools as Agents for Urban Revitalization, Roy Strickland

The registered trademark City of Learning is owned by Roy Strickland.

1 As part of NASDP's field research, more than 100 primary and secondary schools (public, private, parochial, and charter) have been observed in operation in localities such as Berkeley, Oakland, and San Francisco, California; Baltimore, Maryland; Belmont, Boston, Brookline, Cambridge, and Worcester, Massachusetts; Dearborn and Detroit, Michigan; Chicago, Illinois; Philadelphia, Pennsylvania; New York, New York; Paterson, Union City, and Trenton, New Jersey; and Washington, D.C.

2 Dewey's *School and Society* provides diagrams proposing a seamless educational setting. Here schools extend to the "natural environment" and "all its facts and forces," to business and "the needs and forces of industry," and to the home, where a "free interplay of influences, materials, and ideals occurs." Martin S. Dworkin, ed., *Dewey on Education* (New York: Teachers College Press, 1950), 75–78. For Howard Gardner, the ideal school turns to its surroundings for "contextual exploring and learning," with portions of the students' day spent in frequent visits to theaters, symphonies, and art museums and at workplaces under the tutelage of "masters." Howard Gardner, *Multiple Intelligences: The Theory and Practice* (New York: Basic Books, 1993), 68–80.

3 NASDP executed the Union City and Paterson projects. A consultant team consisting of Roy Strickland and ICON Architects executed the project in Trenton.

4 Michael Casey, "Change in Store for Paterson Mall," *The Bergen Record*, July 22, 1999, L–1.

5 Application for Smart Growth Community School Planning Grant, submitted by City of Paterson and Paterson Public Schools to the New Jersey Department of Community Affairs, Office of State Planning, November 15, 2001.

6 At the time of this writing, campus "entry" signage is planned for the North and South State Street entries into campus. This design was done by others and not endorsed in the 1999 Landscape Master Plan.

Education and the Urban Landscape: Illinois Institute of Technology, Peter Lindsay Schaudt

1 Thank you to Chandra Goldsmith and Patricia Uribe for their assistance in the writing of this piece. An earlier version of this piece, "Rehabilitation in Context: Alfred Caldwell's Planting Design for the Illinois Institute of Technology— Rediscovered and Interpreted," was published in: *Vineyard: An Occasional Record of the National Park Service Historic Landscape Initiative* II (2000): 11–13.

2 Phyllis Lambert, Learning a Language," in *Mies in America* (New York: Harry N. Abrams, Inc., 2001), 275.

3 Daniel Bluestone, *Constructing Chicago* (New Haven: Yale University Press, 1991), 52.

4 Construction was finished in the summer of 2001 at a cost of approximately $4.2 million. The campus is now experiencing a renaissance of renewal and restoration. Two distinguished alumni have created a matching fund endowment of $120 million for the historic Mies van der Rohe building restoration and landscape improvements.

5 Peter Carter, *Mies van der Rohe at Work*, quoted in Phyllis Lambert, "Mies and His Colleagues," in *Mies in America* (New York: Harry N. Abrams, Inc., 2001), 583.